BOREDOM
BUSTERS

BOREDOM BUSTERS

Over **50** AWESOME activities for children aged 7 years +

Caroline Fernandez

CICO **kidz**

For Emilie, Chloé, and Tomás.

Acknowledgments

I would like to express my gratitude to the team at CICO Books who helped bring this book to life (and to bookstores!) Specifically, I would like to thank Cindy Richards for making the brave decision to publish me, Carmel Edmonds for her amazing editorial guidance, and Katie Hardwicke for her keen attention to detail.

Above all, I would like to thank my husband Patrick, my parents, and my family, who supported and inspired me throughout the creation of this book.

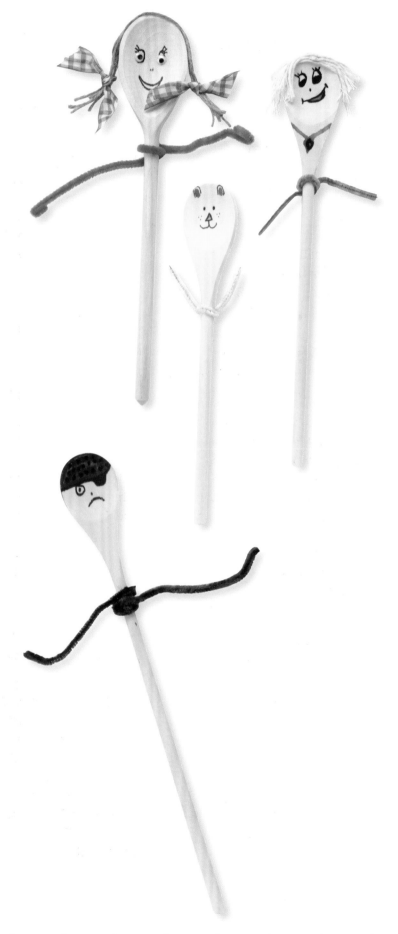

Published in 2014 by CICO Books
An imprint of Ryland Peters & Small
519 Broadway, 5th Floor, New York NY 10012
20–21 Jockey's Fields, London WC1R 4BW
www.rylandpeters.com

10 9 8 7 6 5 4 3 2 1

A CIP catalog record for this book is available from the Library of Congress and the British Library.

ISBN: 978-1-78249-105-7

Printed in China

Editor: Katie Hardwicke
Designer: Isobel Gillan
Photographer: Martin Norris
Stylist: Sophie Martell

Contents

Introduction

Boredom Busters are stress-free, hands-on activities to entertain young readers, using simple materials found around the home or classroom. Activities are organized into five themed sections: Art, Craft, Science, Food, and Travel.

Included are simple yet sensational activities to occupy kids whether they have a few spare minutes while waiting for dinner, need a rainy day project, or want something to do during a long road trip. These activities are great ways to entertain kids without screens; doing something fun and engaging while instilling a sense of personal pride in a finished project. All of the projects are un-competitive and focus on children doing their personal best in each activity. Every Boredom Buster in this book has been kid-tested and kid-approved.

 Several projects are flagged as "eco-friendly," helping to promote recycling and reusing materials rather than buying them.

Guess What...

Each project has a Guess What? feature connected to it. These features are provided for kids to "think outside the box" when they do an activity, giving them tidbits of history, geography, science, and more, which are connected to a specific part of the activity. This makes every Boredom Buster not only entertaining but a bit educational, too (sshhh ...don't tell the kids!).

Learning Skills Developed with Boredom Busters

- Reading (silently and out loud)
- Vocabulary development (what does effervescent mean?)
- Math skills (using a ruler or measuring ingredients)
- Decision making (which activity will you do today?)
- Problem solving (I can't find the scissors!)
- Hand-eye coordination (pouring liquids or placing tape on an item)
- Concentration (paying attention to the activity)
- Patience (waiting for a result)
- Following directions (doing the steps of an activity in the right order)
- Creativity (blending colors or creating a game)
- Gross motor skills (shaking or rolling)
- Fine motor skills (grasping a spoon or holding a paintbrush)

All of the Boredom Buster activities can be done individually. However, you can also do them as group projects with friends or classmates, or as an activity at a party. To make the group activity experience more enjoyable, remember to take turns: divide up the activity responsibilities so it is clear who does what. For example, if you are cooking, one child could be in charge of wet ingredients and another child could be in charge of dry ingredients.

At the start of the projects you'll find a guide to how long each activity takes and its Boredom Buster rating: many activities are one-offs but can always be made again and again. Each project has also been given an activity level rating from one to three stars as a guide to how simple ⭐ or involved ⭐⭐⭐ it is.

BOREDOM BUSTERS TIPS

✓ READ the whole project first before you start to DO the activity

✓ WASH YOUR HANDS before and after every activity

✓ PUT OUT the things that you will need for the activity before you start

✓ COVER your activity area with an activity mat or newspaper to avoid mess

✓ ROLL UP YOUR SLEEVES, tie up your hair, and put on an apron to protect yourself

✓ DO ONE STEP AT A TIME and follow the instructions in order

✓ KEEP your activity and supplies safe —put them on a flat, high surface away from the curious hands of little brothers or sisters. Small items can be choking dangers to young children

✓ WATCH for the stop sign. When you see it, it means stop and ask an adult for help

✓ BE SAFE and keep activities out of reach of small children

✓ DON'T RUSH an activity—be sure to take your time and enjoy the experience

✓ CLEAN UP after you do an activity

CHAPTER 1
Art Activities

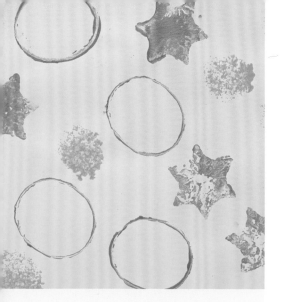

Homemade Stamps

A much-loved activity for instant fun, homemade stamps are great for kids of all ages! You don't have to be an artist to stamp with paint and it doesn't have to look like a specific thing at the end. Stamp with your eyes closed, stamp to music, stamp sitting down, stamp standing up—you can have a different stamping activity every time!

MAKE IT IN: **20 minutes**
BOREDOM BUSTER: **Over and over again**
ACTIVITY LEVEL: ★

Things you need:

- Activity mat or old newspaper
- Apron or old T-shirt
- Homemade stamps: try fruit or vegetables cut in half; bottle tops, cardboard tubes, plastic bottle bases
- Knife
- Cutting board
- Cookie cutter shape (optional)
- Paint: you could use **Homemade Paint** on page 18
- Paper plate
- Paper for printing on

1 Protect your activity surface by putting down an art mat or some newspaper. Tie up your hair, roll up your sleeves, and put on an apron to protect your clothes.

Stop for safety!
Ask an adult to help with cutting.

2 Start by preparing your stamps. If you are using a potato or fruit, ask an adult to help you to cut it on a cutting board. Potatoes, apples, pears, and other fruit can be cut lengthwise or widthwise to give a good surface and different shapes to print from.

3 You can also cut a shape into a potato, if you like. Using a small, shaped cookie cutter, like a flower or a star, press the cookie cutter into the cut side of the potato so that it is pushed in a little. Now carefully cut away the potato around the outside of the shape.

4 Pour some paint onto a paper plate. Put a piece of paper down on your art mat. Dip the stamp into the paint, making sure that it is fully covered, then print on the paper by pressing the stamp lightly—don't wiggle it around too much and try to lift it straight up and off the paper to stop it from smudging.

5 Keep stamping, adding more paint when you need to. You can stamp in lines or patterns, or completely randomly!

6 What shapes do you see with your homemade stamps? Were they the shapes you expected to see? Were you surprised by the shapes?

Guess What...
Potatoes

Potatoes are the fourth largest food crop in the world (No. 1 rice, No. 2, wheat, No. 3 corn). Potatoes are grown all over the world. Potatoes are best kept, at home, in a paper bag in a cool dark place.

English: Potato
French: Pomme de Terre
Spanish: Patata

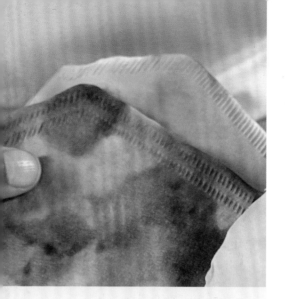

Coffee Filter Watercolors

What happens when you decide to color on paper coffee filters using markers and by accident you spill some water on it? You discover a whole new activity called: Coffee Filter Watercolors! A watercolor is both an art and a science activity—you create a beautiful painting and you observe what happens when colors blend together.

MAKE IT IN: **20 minutes**
BOREDOM BUSTER: **One time activity (but keeps forever)**
ACTIVITY LEVEL: ★

Things you need:

- Activity mat or cookie (baking) sheet lined with wax paper (don't use newspaper—it will get wet!)
- Paper coffee filters (white work best)
- Washable marker pens or felt-tipped pens in 2 or 3 different colors
- A small bowl of water

1 Protect your activity surface by putting down an activity mat or using a lined cookie (baking) sheet. Put a paper coffee filter on the activity mat.

2 Color the coffee filter (on both sides) with markers. You don't need to draw an image, just fill the space with different sections of colors.

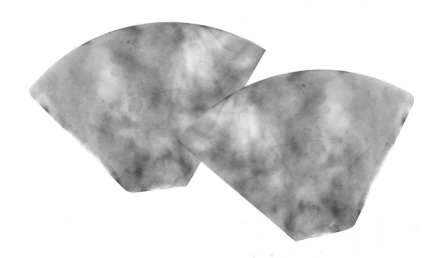

3 Fill a small bowl with water, roll up your sleeves, and dip your fingertips in the water. Sprinkle a little water on the coffee filter by flicking your fingers—do this slowly, over and over again.

Guess What... Coffee Filters

Paper coffee filters were invented by a housewife from Germany in about 1908. The inventor, Melitta Bentz, was tired of finding ground bits of coffee in the bottom of her coffee cup so she went about trying to discover a better way to make coffee. She took some of her son's school paper, cut a circle, put the coffee grounds inside of it, and poured hot water over the coffee and into her cup. The paper filtered the liquid—keeping the coffee bits on top and transforming the liquid into coffee underneath. From this simple experiment she invented coffee filters!

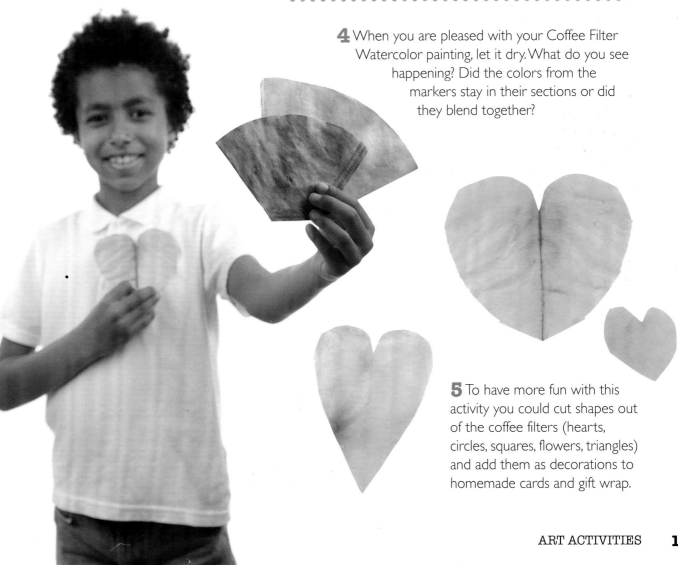

4 When you are pleased with your Coffee Filter Watercolor painting, let it dry. What do you see happening? Did the colors from the markers stay in their sections or did they blend together?

5 To have more fun with this activity you could cut shapes out of the coffee filters (hearts, circles, squares, flowers, triangles) and add them as decorations to homemade cards and gift wrap.

Wax Paper Window Pictures

Decorate the windows of your home or classroom with these easy pictures and wait for the sun to shine through, just like stained glass. What is stained glass, you ask? You may have seen stained glass at a castle, church, or museum where some of the windows have colorful pictures in the glass.

MAKE IT IN: 20 minutes
BOREDOM BUSTER: One time activity (but keeps forever)
ACTIVITY LEVEL: ★★

Things you need:

- Iron and ironing board
- Scissors
- Wax paper
- Art pieces, like fresh or dry leaves, dried flowers and petals, or colored tissue paper (make sure the art pieces are thin)
- Dish (tea) towel
- Sticky tape

1 Ask an adult to help you to plug in the iron and turn it to the warm setting.

2 Using scissors, cut two pieces of wax paper approximately the same size. Use a standard size piece of paper to draw around, if you like.

Stop for safety!
Ask an adult to help you with the hot iron.

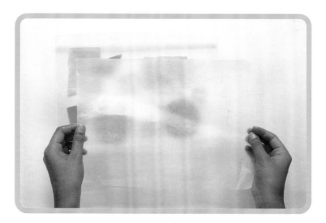

3 Lay out your art pieces—let's say for this activity you are using tissue paper. Lay out the pieces of tissue paper across one sheet of wax paper in any order you like—you can make them into a picture, a pattern, or leave them in a natural arrangement. Next, cover the tissue paper pieces with the second piece of wax paper, taking care not to move your arrangement.

4 Cover the wax paper with a dish (tea) towel, then slowly and gently iron the tea towel. The heat from the iron will melt the wax, binding the wax paper layers together. You do NOT want to iron directly on the wax paper because the wax will melt onto the iron, which is why you put a dish towel on top! If you're using dried petals or leaves, don't worry if you hear them crunching a little—they will survive!

5 Allow the wax paper to cool. Using scissors, trim off any rough or uneven edges.

6 Use little pieces of tape to stick your window art to your window.

Guess What...
Wax Paper

Wax paper is paper that is coated with a thin layer of wax making it water-resistant. Wax paper can be used to grease baking pans with butter, wrap cookies, and as a funnel to transfer things from one place to another (like small beads into a glass jar). Wax paper cannot be recycled because of chemicals added to it during its creation.

Recycled Crayon Necklace

Turn your old odds and ends of broken or used crayons into something completely different! This pretty pendant is one idea but you could also recycle the crayons into a whole new set of art supplies—great for future art projects and nice enough to give as gifts to friends and teachers.

 Recycle little bits of old crayons into new supplies.

MAKE IT IN: **30 minutes**
BOREDOM BUSTER: **One time activity (but keeps forever)**
ACTIVITY LEVEL: ★ ★ ★

Things you need:

- Crayon pieces with the paper labels removed
- Metal cupcake pan
- Paper cupcake liners
- Oven mitts
- Cooling rack
- Drinking straw
- String or ribbon

 ## More shape ideas:

Create other shapes using different-shaped baking pans, like mini loaf pans to make rectangles.

1 Ask an adult to help you to turn the oven on to 200°F (95°C/Gas ¼) to preheat.

Stop for safety!
Ask an adult to help you with the oven.

2 Make sure all the paper labels are peeled off your previously loved, broken crayons. Break the crayons into pieces of different sizes (just snap them using your fingers).

3 Put the paper cupcake liners in the cupcake pan, then add a few broken crayon pieces to each liner so that it is a quarter to half full, depending on how thick you want your pendant or new crayons.

4 Put on the oven mitts and ask an adult to help you put the cupcake pan in the oven. Bake the crayons in the oven for 8–10 minutes, or until the crayons are fully melted.

5 Use the oven mitts to remove the cupcake pan and set it on a wire cooling rack. Do not touch the melted crayons until they are completely cool.

Guess what... Crayons

A crayon is made by adding color to wax. Crayons are used throughout the world for arts and crafts. It is thought that the word "crayon" comes from "craie," the French word for chalk.

English: crayons
French: crayons de couleur
Spanish: lápices

6 To make a hole to hang your pendant from, poke a short piece of drinking straw into the melted crayon while it is still liquid. When set, pull out the straw—it will leave a hole.

7 Thread a piece of string or ribbon through the hole and you've created a Recycled Crayon Necklace!

8 For crayons, simply unpeel the paper cupcake liner from your new crayon and you are ready to color.

Homemade Paint

Out of paint? No worries! This easy homemade paint is a fast, no-cook activity that will have you ready to be creative in 5 minutes. Homemade paint is a little more watery than store-bought paint (but it works great). This activity makes one pot of homemade paint. To make different colors, repeat the activity using the same ingredients and use different shades of food coloring each time.

 Recycle plastic food containers into paint pots.

MAKE IT IN: **5 minutes**
BOREDOM BUSTER: **One time activity (but you can make more with the ingredients)**
ACTIVITY LEVEL: ★

Things you need:

- Activity mat or old newspaper
- Apron or old T-shirt
- Measuring cup
- 2 tbsp flour
- 4 tbsp water
- 1 tbsp salt
- Bowl
- Spoon
- Food coloring in red, blue, yellow, and green
- Paint pots: clean and re-use applesauce or yogurt containers

1 Protect your activity surface by putting down an activity mat or some newspaper. Tie up your hair, roll up your sleeves, and put on an apron or old T-shirt to protect your clothes.

2 Measure the flour, water, and salt into a bowl and mix them all together with a spoon.

3 Now add a few drops of food coloring: use about 5 drops for light colors and 10 drops for bolder colors.

4 Stir well, then transfer to a clean paint pot. Repeat to make more colors, then grab a paintbrush, and get painting! You could use your Homemade Paint in the Hand Print Art activity on page 20, too.

Make your own paint colors...

Most food coloring comes in the standard colors of red, blue, and yellow. You can mix these 3 basic colors to create even more...

red + yellow = orange

yellow + blue = green

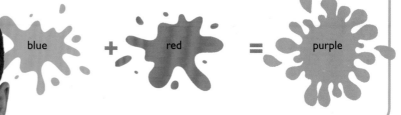

blue + red = purple

Guess What...
Food Coloring

Food coloring stains hands and clothes because it is a man-made dye, which has been especially manufactured to change the color of things. Food coloring is often used in baking to change the color of frosting. It can also be used to make fake blood for movies, plays, and television shows.

Hand Print Art

Ready to be artistic but don't have a paintbrush? What about hand print art?! For this activity, your hands are your main tool, so be sure to roll up your sleeves! Fun to do and easy to make, hand print art is really unique!

MAKE IT IN: 20 minutes
BOREDOM BUSTER: One time activity (but keeps forever)
ACTIVITY LEVEL: ★

. . . .

Things you need:

- Activity mat or old newspaper
- Apron or old T-shirt
- Paint: use **Homemade Paint** on page 18 or store-bought washable craft paint
- Paper: use either printer paper or construction paper of any color
- Paper plate or a large container big enough to dip your whole hand into
- Black felt-tipped marker pen

1 Protect your activity surface by putting down an activity mat or some newspaper. Tie up your hair, roll up your sleeves, and put on an apron or old T-shirt to protect your clothes.

2 Pour some paint onto the paper plate or container. Dip the flat of your hand in the paint—imagine you are giving the paint a high-five!

Guess What... Paint

Paint has been around for centuries. Ancient caves with painted walls have been discovered in France and Spain—some of the cave paintings even feature hand print art, just like yours! Ancient Egyptians painted tombs, temples, and palaces of the Pharaohs (Egyptian royalty). Native peoples painted their faces as symbols—red for war, white for peace, and yellow for death. Today, we use paint to decorate many things: cars, walls, furniture, clothes, and much, much more!

3 Now lower your painted hand flat onto the paper. Press firmly (without wriggling!).

4 Quickly release your hand from the paper, leaving your hand print behind. See left for some ideas on turning your hand print into a picture using a marker pen.

5 What does the paint on your hand feel like? Is it wet or dry? Squishy or firm?

More hand print art ideas:

- *Hand print flower: hand print with fingers pointing up. Use a marker to draw a stem and leaves.*

- *Hand print fish: hand print with fingers pointing to the right. Use a marker to draw eyes and mouth on the palm.*

- *Hand print tree: make five hand prints with fingers pointing up: three hand prints on bottom, then two in the middle and one on the top.*

- *Hand print elephant: hand print with fingers pointing down so that the thumb is a trunk. Use a marker to draw the eye, ear, and tail.*

- *You could also try this activity with fabric paint and print your own T-shirts!*

Magazine Mosaic

Is your recycling bin full of magazines that have been read and are no longer needed? You can transform them into a neat art project (or several art projects). This magazine mosaic creates a rainbow of eco-friendly artwork.

Recycle old magazines into colorful art.

MAKE IT IN: **15 minutes**
BOREDOM BUSTER: **One time activity (but keeps forever)**
ACTIVITY LEVEL: ★

Things you need:

- Old magazine(s)—make sure everyone has finished reading them first
- Scissors
- Marker pen
- Art paper or a paper plate
- Glue

1 Cut out lots of small squares from the magazine pages, all the same size, and group them in colors: blue, red, yellow, green.

2 Then, using a marker pen, draw a picture on the art paper or paper plate. Why not try the sun, sky, waves, a flower, or a rainbow? Or you could draw an abstract shape, like a spiral.

Guess What... Mosaic

A mosaic is a picture made up of many small squares. The Ancient Romans created mosaics to decorate walls and floors. Mosaics can also be made by creating a picture with tiny squares of colored glass or tiles and setting them in plaster.

3 Put the colored squares of paper on the paper by following your marker lines as a template. Add the squares, one by one, grouping them by color.

More mosaic art ideas:

Another great idea is to make a word cloud—a cluster of single words put together in an artwork. You can group Word Cloud Magazine Mosaics by categories like: Love, Friends, Life, Family, or Sports. Find words from a category in magazine titles and articles, and cut them out. So, for Family, look for: sister, baby, brother, Mom, Dad, home, love, laugh, and so on. Then, paste the words onto an art paper, making a word cloud.

4 Now glue the colored squares in place. Continue until you have covered the art paper and the guidelines in a mosaic.

5 Ta-daaa! Your Magazine Mosaic is done.

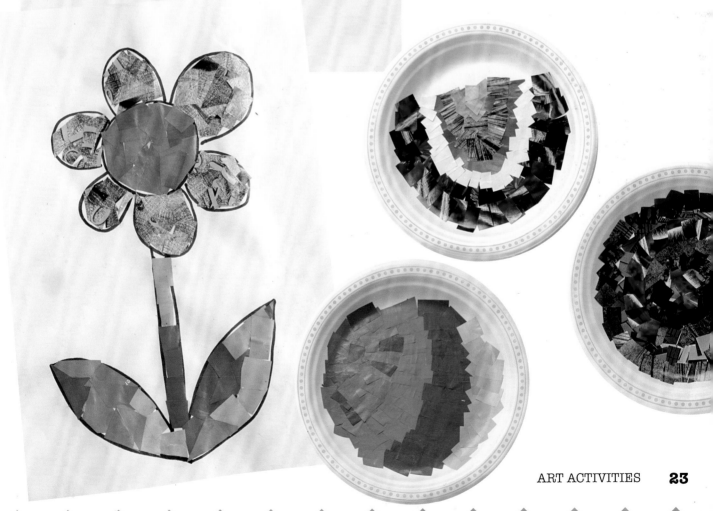

Shaving Cream Art

This colorful creation is just plain cool! A great activity for birthday parties, a pastime on vacation, or a simple project for an afternoon art attack, this painting is permanent (it lasts forever) and is never the same twice. If you are doing Shaving Cream Art as your birthday party activity, send the finished paintings home as part of the loot bags for your guests.

MAKE IT IN: **15 minutes**
BOREDOM BUSTER: **One time activity (but keeps forever)**
ACTIVITY LEVEL: ★

Things you need:

- Activity mat or old newspaper
- Apron
- Art canvas (available at discount stores and art or craft stores)
- Shaving cream (ask Dad first!)
- Food coloring: choose 4 or 5 different colors
- Spoon
- Paper napkin or paper (kitchen) towel

1 Protect your activity surface by putting down an art mat or some newspaper. Tie up your hair, roll up your sleeves, and put on an apron to protect your clothes.

Stop for safety!
Ask an adult to supervise spraying of shaving cream.

2 Put the canvas on your activity mat and spray a circle of shaving cream about the size of your palm (the underneath part of your hand) in the center of the canvas.

3 Next, add about four drops of food coloring (using four or five different colors) in random parts of the shaving cream. Some drops up, some drops down, some left, some right. The coloring will stain the canvas almost instantly, so work the next step quickly.

4 Now hold the spoon upside down so that the bowl is in your hand and the handle is pointed toward the art canvas. Using the handle as your paintbrush, drag the shaving cream around the canvas—try "drawing" lines, swirls, or circles. Don't mix too much—the colors will blend together and make gray!

5 When you're happy with the effect, take your canvas to the garbage (rubbish) bin and use the spoon to wipe the shaving cream off the canvas and into the bin. Wipe any remaining shaving cream off using a paper napkin or paper (kitchen) towel.

Guess What...
Shaving Cream

Shaving cream is made out of oils, soaps, water, and other ingredients to help prepare skin for shaving and to protect against cuts. Men have been shaving for centuries but not just their faces. Ancient Egyptian, Greek, and Roman soldiers all shaved their heads to protect themselves from enemies pulling their hair in battle.

6 You will be left with a finished, colorful artwork! What do you see on your art canvas? What happened to the food coloring? Why do you think that happened? The food coloring sinks beneath the shaving cream and stains the art canvas making it a one-of-a-kind piece of artwork.

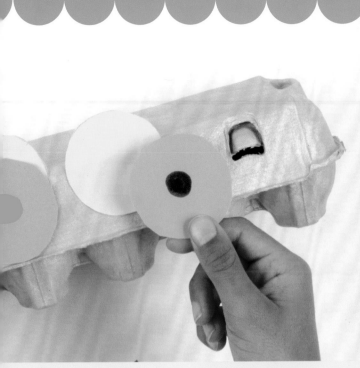

CHAPTER 2
Craft Activities

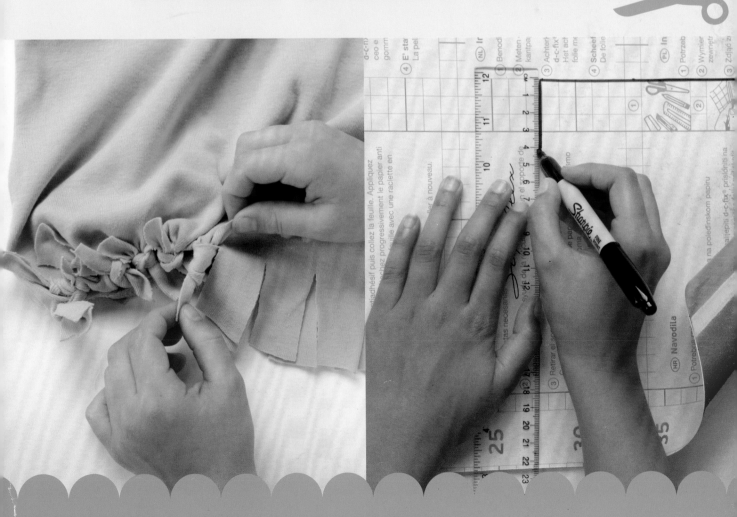

Egg Carton Creature

Do you ever need a place to hold your teeny tiny stuff? Recycle a cardboard egg carton to make a fun tidy to hold erasers, hair ties, stickers, buttons, jewelry, craft supplies, or whatever other itsy bitsy gear you have on hand. This is a great 2-in-1 activity, as you are not only making an organizer for yourself but also creating an egg carton creature to decorate your desk.

Give a new purpose to something from the recycling bin.

MAKE IT IN: **1 hour**
BOREDOM BUSTER: **One time activity (but keeps forever)**
ACTIVITY LEVEL: ★

Things you need:

- Art mat or old newspaper
- Apron
- Acrylic paint
- A cardboard egg carton
- Paper plate
- Paintbrush
- Pencil and colored paper
- Scissors
- Marker pens or felt-tipped pens
- Glue

1 Protect your activity surface with an activity mat or newspapers. Roll up your sleeves and put on an apron to protect your clothes.

2 Pour some paint onto a paper plate and, holding the egg carton over the activity mat, paint the egg carton all over, top and bottom. Let the egg carton dry.

Guess What... Egg Cartons

The egg carton was invented by Joseph Coyle of British Columbia, Canada, in 1911. He invented the egg carton to solve a disagreement between a local egg farmer and hotel owner. The hotel owner and farmer were both angry that eggs kept getting broken during their journey from the farm to the hotel. So Joseph invented a paper carton to protect the fragile eggs during transport.

3 In the meantime, draw eyes and teeth on colored paper. To help you draw circles, use a small pot, button, or lid to draw round. Make two sets of eyes on different colored paper then cut them out, along with the teeth.

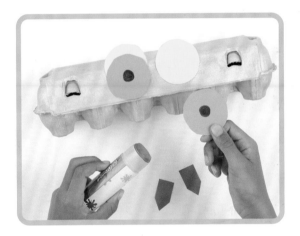

5 When the paint on the egg carton is dry, glue on the eyes and teeth in the middle of the front edge, creating the face of your Egg Carton Creature. Open his jaws wide and your desk-pet is ready to use!

4 Using a marker pen or felt-tipped pen, draw the pupils in the middle of the eyes. Position the pupils in different places to give your creature a fun expression.

Papier-mâché Bowl

Transform newspapers that have been read into a useful bowl.

MAKE IT IN: **48 hours (to allow time to set)**

BOREDOM BUSTER: **One time activity (but keeps forever)**

ACTIVITY LEVEL: ★ ★

Named after the French term for "chewed paper," papier-mâché crafts reuse old newspaper. Papier mâché can be used to make masks, puppets, animal figures, and more. A bit messy (but messy is fun, isn't it?), this activity is great for spending a bit of time crafting, and you get a really useful bowl for storing all your bits and pieces, too!

1 Protect your activity surface by putting down an activity mat or some newspaper. Tie up your hair, roll up your sleeves, and put on an apron to protect your clothes. Add the flour and water to a bowl and mix in the salt (this helps to prevent mold).

You can't eat out of a papier-mâché bowl—it is for decoration and organization only!

2 Mix well, using a spoon, until there are no lumps. The mixture should have the consistency of glue; add a little more water or flour if you need to.

Things you need:

- Activity mat or old newspaper
- Apron
- 2 bowls: one for mixing ingredients and one to hold the balloon
- Measuring cup
- 1 cup (230 g) flour
- 2 cups (500 ml) water
- 1 tbsp salt
- Spoon
- Balloon
- Old newspaper torn into strips: enough to cover half the balloon
- Craft paint or **Homemade Paint** (see page 18)
- Beads or jewels to decorate (optional)

More papier-mâché ideas:

Blow up balloons to other sizes to make different-sized bowls.

Guess What... Papier-mâché Festival

Las Fallas is a festival that happens every year in Valencia, Spain, where neighborhoods parade giant papier-mâché figures (often 20 feet/6 meters tall!) around the streets. Artists make the papier-mâché characters (often looking like giants). Tourists come from far and wide to see the colossal papier-mâché models!

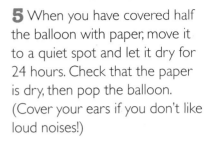

5 When you have covered half the balloon with paper, move it to a quiet spot and let it dry for 24 hours. Check that the paper is dry, then pop the balloon. (Cover your ears if you don't like loud noises!)

3 Blow up the balloon, tie a knot in the end, and place the balloon knot-side-down in the other bowl.

4 Take a few newspaper strips and dip them in the flour and water paste. Strip by strip, cover half of the balloon (criss-crossing and overlapping the paper will make it stronger). Smooth the strips down as you go to get an even surface.

6 You can now paint and decorate your bowl as you like: why not match it to your bedroom colors, or make one as a gift for your mom or a friend? Paint the inside of the bowl and then the outside.

7 Let the paint dry for another 24 hours before using the bowl or adding a few decorations, like beads or jewels.

Milk Jug Monster Bowling Pins

Clean and save your plastic milk jugs. Why? Well, plastic milk jugs make perfect bowling pins. Milk jug bowling is great for outdoor play as well as indoor fun. Play by yourself or with your friends. Remember to gently "roll" the ball, you don't need to throw or toss it—champion bowlers are really skilled at controlling the ball!

Keep landfills clear by recycling plastic milk jugs.

MAKE IT IN: **5 minutes**
BOREDOM BUSTER: **One time activity (but you can play it over and over again)**
ACTIVITY LEVEL: ★

Things you need:

• Clean, plastic milk jugs: any size you like and as many as you like
• Permanent marker pens
• Googly craft eyes (optional)
• Tennis ball or any small ball

1 Make sure your milk jugs are all clean. With the milk jug right way up (pouring end up!), draw a monster face in the middle of the jug (you can draw a face on both sides, if you like). Angry face, happy face, silly face, surprised face… It's up to you. Add extra eyes, hair, hats, or glasses, if you like.

2 Once you're happy with the monster's face, color in the features in different colors to make them bright and show up well. If you make a mistake, you can remove permanent marker with a little rubbing alcohol and start again.

3 If you like, stick some googly craft eyes onto your monster— they'll wobble when he wobbles!

4 Place the jugs at one end of a hallway or room and walk to the opposite end, or at the end of the yard or path if you're playing outside.

5 Gently (we don't want to break anything!) roll the ball toward the monster milk jugs to knock them down, just like bowling pins.

6 Strike! You can mark numbers on the bottoms of the jugs if you would like to keep score (10 points, 5 points, 2 points), although just knocking the pins down is much more fun than winning!

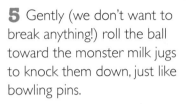

Guess What...
Milk Jugs

Milk jugs take up a lot of space in landfills. Approximately 16,000 large (4 liter) milk jugs make up one tonne of bulky garbage. Milk jugs are made from high-density polyethylene plastic, which makes them perfect for recycling. The plastic can be recycled into other plastic items like plastic pipes, toys, flower pots, and patio furniture.

Baby Food Jar Snow Globe

Do you have a baby brother or sister, or are you a babysitter or know of a family with a baby? If so, you can collect, clean, and recycle a baby food jar into a made-it-yourself snow globe. It looks great as a desk decoration or paperweight.

 Give empty baby food jars a new purpose.

MAKE IT IN: **2 hours**
BOREDOM BUSTER: **One time activity (but keeps forever)**
ACTIVITY LEVEL: ★ ★ ★

Things you need:

- A glass baby food jar with lid
- A glueable figurine (plastic, crystal, or ceramic), ideally with a flat base, that is shorter than your jar
- Waterproof superglue
- Glitter
- Water

1 Take the lid off the jar and ask an adult to help you to superglue the figurine to the inside of the lid. Set aside to let it dry.

2 Fill the jar three-quarters full with water, then add about half a teaspoon of glitter.

3 Carefully put the lid on the jar, inserting the figurine as you go. Ask an adult to help you to apply superglue around the lid to seal it. DO NOT TURN OVER YET. Put the jar to one side, out of the way, and wait for the glue to dry.

4 Shake the Baby Jar Snow Globe and watch the glitter shower down around your figurine!

Guess What...
Snow Globes

Usually made of glass in a dome-like shape, snow globes are also known as snow domes and water globes. Snow globes have been sold since the late 1800s. In the 1950s, manufacturers starting selling them with plastic domes instead of glass, making them less fragile.

Homemade Hobo Bag

MAKE IT IN: **30 minutes**
BOREDOM BUSTER: **One time activity (but keeps forever)**
ACTIVITY LEVEL: ★ ★ ★

Hobo bags are really trendy these days. From a school bag to activity bag to book bag, the hobo is a hit! Also, it's a great birthday party activity—making a Homemade Hobo Bag is an easy, hands-on activity and makes a great loot bag. Always check with an adult before cutting up any of your T-shirts!

Things you need:

- A clean T-shirt (check you have permission to use it)
- Scissors: fabric scissors work best
- Marker pens (optional)

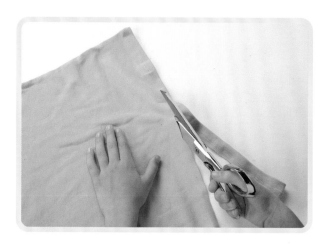

1 Lay your T-shirt out on a flat surface, like a table. Cut off the bottom hem through both layers—use the stitching on the hem as a guide. Don't worry too much about cutting a straight line, the cotton fabric from the T-shirt will roll a bit at the cut edges to hide any jagged cuts. Put the hem aside, it will become the strap to the bag!

2 Cut slits along the bottom of the T-shirt, about 2in (5cm) long and about 1in (2.5cm) apart.

3 Starting at the side seam, double knot the matching top and bottom strips together, working your way along the bottom to seal the base of the bag.

4 Stretch the bottom of the bag to put it back to a square shape (you might hear some ripping—that's OK!).

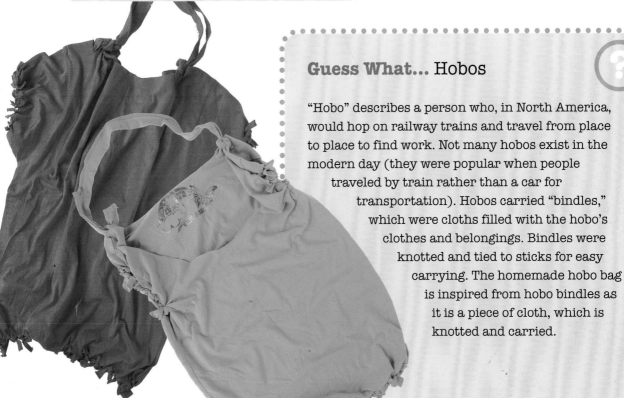

Guess What... Hobos

"Hobo" describes a person who, in North America, would hop on railway trains and travel from place to place to find work. Not many hobos exist in the modern day (they were popular when people traveled by train rather than a car for transportation). Hobos carried "bindles," which were cloths filled with the hobo's clothes and belongings. Bindles were knotted and tied to sticks for easy carrying. The homemade hobo bag is inspired from hobo bindles as it is a piece of cloth, which is knotted and carried.

5 On the sleeves, cut through both layers just above the hems. Now cut slits in the arms as you did in step 2 and double knot the top and bottom pieces of fabric together as in step 3.

6 Now cut just below the hem on the neckline through both the top and bottom layers of fabric to make the opening for your bag.

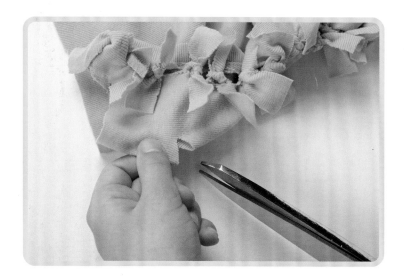

7 Cut a small V-slit in each of the shoulders of the T-shirt. Use the hem that you cut away in step 1 and knot the end through the slits. This creates a shoulder strap fixed to the bag.

8 For a shoulder bag: loop the whole piece (which is in the shape of a circle) through the V-slits and knot. For a longer, cross-body-bag: cut through the hem piece to make one long length, loop the two ends through the V-slits, and knot.

9 If you like, you can decorate your bag with marker pens, permanent or fabric markers, stickers, or glitter glue. Just remember to put a piece of cardboard inside the shirt (between the front and back layers of the shirt) so that markers do not bleed through the fabric.

Rather than throwing old CDs in the trash, recycle them into sparkly discs.

MAKE IT IN: 24 hours
BOREDOM BUSTER: One time activity (but keeps forever)
ACTIVITY LEVEL: ★ ★

Things you need:

- Activity mat, old newspaper, or wax paper
- Scissors
- Cotton string
- An old CD or DVD (check with an adult first!)
- Paper plate
- Glue
- Sparkles or glass beads, you can use lots of different colors if you like

More string ornament ideas:

You could try this activity using colored yarn instead of string, or why not wrap the string around a glass jar and turn it into a cool pencil holder?

Ring of String Ornament

This sparkly, dangly ornament is super easy to make and becomes a great hanging decoration. It's also a fun, hands-on, messy activity—perfect for a rainy day!

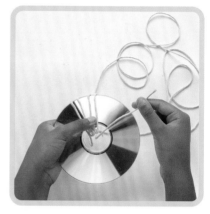

1 Protect your activity surface by putting down an activity mat, some old newspaper, or wax paper. Cut a really, really long piece of string.

2 Insert the string through the CD hole and loop it around. Hold on to the end of the string and continue threading and looping the string through the hole until the CD is completely covered in string.

3 Next, put the string-covered CD on a paper plate. Using your fingers (this is the messy part!) spread glue all over the string and CD (the glue will stick the end of the string so that it won't unravel).

4 Sprinkle sparkles generously over the glue (the paper plate will catch any sprinkles that fall off). Repeat on the other side of the ring of string, spreading glue and adding sparkles.

5 Now let your decorated CD dry for about 24 hours. When dry, loop a piece of string through the center of the CD and tie a knot in the ends. Your Ring of String Ornament is ready to hang!

Guess What...
Ornaments

An ornament is a decoration used to add beauty to a room. In Victorian times, kids made "pomanders" from oranges, tied with a ribbon to hang in their homes. Making orange pomanders is still a great activity: take an orange, poke holes in it, and push cloves into the holes. Tie a ribbon around the orange and hang up to be admired. It will release a lovely, spicy smell—perfect for Christmas festivities.

Plastic Bag Friendship Braid

What can you do with all those plastic bags lying around? What about making friendship braids with them? These braids are easy to do and take just minutes to make. Use the braid as a friendship bracelet, bookmark, or key chain. You can make one for yourself or make a bunch and give them out to all your friends.

Most homes have a collection of plastic bags for recycling so you're sure to find a bag or two for this project.

MAKE IT IN: **10 minutes**
BOREDOM BUSTER: **Over and over again**
ACTIVITY LEVEL: ★

Things you need:

• Plastic bag, or bags in different colors
• Scissors

1 Cut the plastic bag into strips with scissors. Make the strips as long as the bag and about 1in (2.5cm) wide.

2 Take three strips all the same length and knot them together at one end. If you like, you can ask a friend to hold one end while you braid (plait) the strips.

3 Braid (plait) the three strips tightly: take the right strip and cross it over the center, then take the left strip and cross it over the center. Continue until your braid is complete.

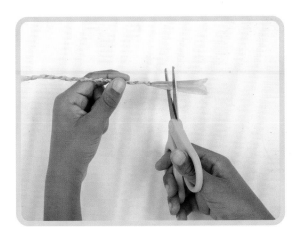

4 Tie a knot at the other end of your braid then use scissors to cut off any extra bits at the ends.

Guess What...
Plastic Bags

Scientists believe it takes about 450 to 1,000 years for plastic bags to break down in landfills. Many marine animals die when they become tangled in bags or mistake plastic bags for food. So it's really important to recycle plastic bags and try to use fewer bags at the supermarket when you can.

5 Your Plastic Bag Friendship Braid is done! To make a bracelet, simply tie the two ends together. For a really colorful version, use strips from different colored plastic bags.

Cinnamon Clay

MAKE IT IN: **24 hours**
BOREDOM BUSTER: **One time activity (but keeps for months)**
ACTIVITY LEVEL: ★★

A favorite activity, this cinnamon clay is great to sculpt and smells super nice! Roll, pat, and shape for hands-on fun! As the clay dries it will harden and then keep for months. You will want one in every room of your house! Cinnamon Clay makes a great gift as a present for your teacher or for Mother's Day, Father's Day, or Valentine's Day!

Things you need:

- Activity mat (or cookie/baking sheet)
- Apron
- Wax paper
- 1 cup (250 g) applesauce
- 1 cup (120 g) ground cinnamon
- Medium-sized bowl
- Wooden spoon
- Rolling pin and cookie cutters (optional)
- Drinking straw
- Cooling rack
- Ribbon

1 Protect your activity surface by putting down an activity mat or a cookie (baking) sheet. Tie up your hair, roll up your sleeves, and put on an apron to protect your clothes. Cut a sheet of wax paper and place it on your activity mat or cookie sheet.

2 Measure out the applesauce and cinnamon into a medium-sized bowl, then mix them together well with a wooden spoon.

3 When well combined, remove the cinnamon/applesauce mixture from the bowl and place onto your prepared sheet of wax paper. Press and roll the mixture, using your hands, until it becomes firm clay. What happens when you start pressing the cinnamon mixture with your fingers? Does it fall apart or cling together? Does the cinnamon smell sweet or sour?

4 Now have some fun making or cutting shapes. You can roll the dough out flat using a rolling pin. Younger kids can roll the clay into balls (snake shapes work too!) with their hands or use cookie cutters with adult supervision to cut out shapes.

5 Older kids can use a rolling pin to roll the dough and then use cookie cutters to cut shapes or mold figures or objects.

Guess What... ❓
Cinnamon

Cinnamon was once considered more valuable than gold. It is a spice that comes from cinnamon trees. Cinnamon trees were first found in Sri Lanka but are now also grown in many hot places, such as South America. Cinnamon is often used as a spice in baking, teas, cereals, and soups.

6 Put your finished shapes back on your activity mat. Press a drinking straw through the top of your shape to make a hole for hanging a ribbon through later.

7 Place the Cinnamon Clay decorations on a cooling rack in a warm, dry area—your kitchen table would work fine. Let the Cinnamon Clay decorations dry for about 24 hours, turning occasionally to ensure they dry evenly.

8 When dry, cut a strip of ribbon and loop it through the hole. Tie a knot in the ends and your Cinnamon Clay decoration is ready for hanging.

Duct Tape Lanyard

This lanyard will come in handy on your next trip and you could even use it everyday to keep track of useful stuff. Lanyards can hold a variety of items such as keys, ID tags, whistles, tickets, trading cards, and more. If you want to keep an object with you—and safe—this is a must-do activity.

MAKE IT IN: **25 minutes**
BOREDOM BUSTER: **Over and over again**
ACTIVITY LEVEL: ★★

Things you need:

- Duct tape: look for colorful or patterned tapes in craft or office supply stores
- Ruler
- Scissors
- Hole punch
- Binder clip

More lanyard ideas:

You can switch up the duct tape lanyard by mixing and matching different colors of duct tape. You can make duct tape key chains by doing the same activity but using shorter lengths of duct tape. Make one for anyone going on a trip—it's super handy!

1 Cut one strip of duct tape 18in (46cm) long—measure and mark the tape where you need to cut it. Place the duct tape strip upside down (sticky side UP, otherwise it's going to STICK!) on your work surface.

2 Fold the duct tape in half lengthwise (so that the sticky surface is inside and the colored surface is on the outside). Cut another strip of duct tape 18in (46cm) long and repeat steps 1 and 2 so that you have two strips the same.

Guess What... Lanyards

The word "lanyard" comes from the French word "lanière," meaning "strap." Lanyards are useful because they can easily be attached to—and removed from—any object you wish to keep visible.

3 Next, cut three pieces of duct tape 2in (5cm) long—the tape can be the same or a different color or pattern. Place the small pieces of duct tape upside down (sticky side UP) on your surface.

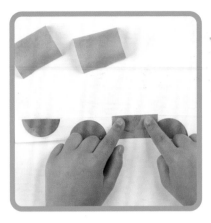

4 Take the two long, folded pieces of duct tape and place them on the sticky side of one small piece with their ends together.

5 Wrap the smaller piece of duct tape around the ends to make one long piece.

6 Now, lay the two open ends on top of each other on the second piece of small tape and wrap it around them to make a loop.

7 Using scissors, trim off any rough edges. Take the hole punch and make one hole in the center of the flat end, about ½in (1.5cm) from the tip. See page 63 for how to clean your scissors if they are sticky.

8 Hook the binder clip through the hole and—voila—your Duct Tape Lanyard is done!

Duct Tape Wallet

This make-it-yourself wallet is super cool. A great place to keep your ID cards, money, coupons, and room cards—this activity is practical and fun! It's a bit tricky working with sticky duct tape but well worth it as this Duct Tape Wallet will last a long, long time.

MAKE IT IN: **15 minutes**
BOREDOM BUSTER: **One time activity (but use over and over again)**
ACTIVITY LEVEL: ★ ★ ★

Things you need:

• Scissors
• Large duct tape
• Ruler

1 Cut 10 strips of duct tape, 8½in (22cm) long. Once you've cut each strip, hang the duct tape pieces off the end of a table to keep them organized and stop them sticking together, or to you!

Guess What... Duct Tape

Duct tape is a super sticky, super strong tape. It is manufactured with a fabric, water-resistant, back. Duct tape now comes in a variety of bold colors and designs. Duct tape was used by American astronauts on the 1970 Apollo 13 space mission. When the crew found themselves in an emergency situation after an on-board explosion, they used duct tape to fix the damaged spaceship parts.

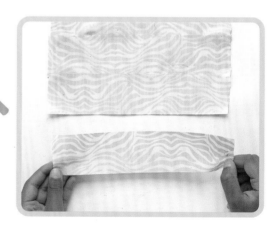

2 Lay one piece of duct tape sticky side up on your activity surface. Place the second piece of duct tape below the first, overlapping the long edges slightly so they stick together.

3 Repeat with three other pieces of duct tape so that you have a rectangle of 5 pieces of tape—stuck together—facing sticky side up.

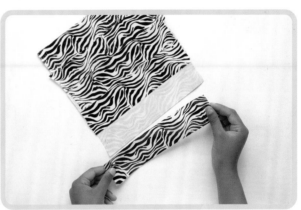

4 Place the next five strips of duct tape, one by one, sticky side down onto the rectangle of duct tape. You will end up with a large rectangle of duct tape fabric.

5 Use your scissors to trim any uneven edges into a straight line. See page 63 for how to clean your scissors if they are sticky.

More duct tape wallet ideas:

Make pockets for your Duct Tape Wallet. Cut two strips of duct tape. Stick them together. Cut this duct tape "fabric" to size, for example you can use your library card as a measurement guide, and tape it into your Duct Tape Wallet, creating inside pockets for your cards.

6 Fold the bottom edge of the rectangle to the top, so that it is folded in half. Press to make a crease in the bottom edge.

7 Cut two pieces of duct tape, 5in (12cm) long. With the rectangle folded in half, place one shorter strip of duct tape along the side, taping the edges closed. Do the same on the other side.

8 Use scissors to trim off any bits of tape that extend beyond the edges.

9 Use your fingers to tuck in any sticky parts still left. Fold the wallet from left to right to make it pocket-sized and you are done!

Activity Bag

Turn a discount store placemat into a cool activity bag to hold your gear. It is great for crayons, paper, toys, and keepsakes. This Activity Bag has many uses and it only takes 15 minutes to make! The bag would also make an easy and budget-friendly loot bag at your next birthday party. You could try it with a round placemat, too.

MAKE IT IN: **15 minutes**
BOREDOM BUSTER: **Over and over again**
ACTIVITY LEVEL: ★ ★

Things you need:

- Discount store placemat: vinyl or fabric are the easiest to wash; avoid plastic mats as they will not bend easily and may have sharp edges
- Adhesive Velcro strips
- Hot glue gun

Stop for safety!
Ask a grown-up to help with the hot glue gun—it can burn.

1 Fold one short end of the placemat up by about one-third and crease it gently.

Guess What... Velcro

Velcro is actually not a thing but a company. Velcro manufactures hook and loop fasteners, which consist of two thin strips of plastic, one strip with tiny loops and a second strip with tiny hooks. The hooks stick to the loops when pressed together and unstick when they are pulled apart.

Hook and loop fasteners have a wide range of uses, from keeping your shoes fastened to securing items on an airplane during take-off.

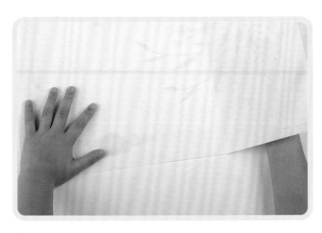

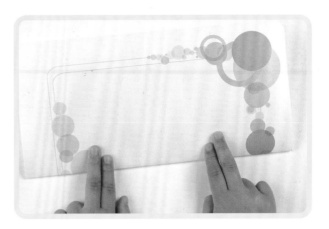

2 Ask an adult to help you use the hot glue gun to apply a thin line of glue along the side edges of the folded section. (Take care—hot glue really does get super hot!) Press the folded section in place and wait for the glue to cool and set.

3 Next, fold the top flap down and make a light crease along the fold.

4 Take a short strip of the adhesive Velcro. To ensure the top and bottom pieces of the Velcro match up in the right spot, keep the Velcro together then place one sticky side of the Velcro on the top of the flap (on the inside), remove the sticker from the underside and then shut the flap closed and press. The bottom of the Velcro will stick in just the right spot.

5 When the glue is cool your Activity Bag is ready to fill.

Cookie Sheet Magnet Board

MAKE IT IN: **20 minutes**
BOREDOM BUSTER: **One
time activity (but keeps
forever)**
ACTIVITY LEVEL: ★

Re-purpose an old, clean, cookie sheet into your personal magnet bulletin board. This provides the perfect way of helping you keep track of school forms, to-do lists, and invitations, as well as giving you a place to display your artwork.

Things you need:

- Cookie (baking) sheet
- Ruler
- Self-adhesive paper or contact paper (available at discount stores and hardware stores)
- Marker pen
- Scissors
- Magnets

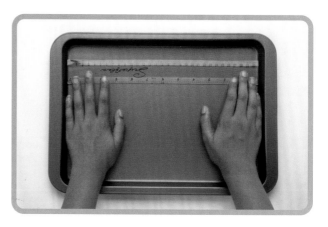

1 Using a ruler, measure the inside dimensions of the cookie sheet (the length and width).

Guess What... Magnets

Magnets are not just for displaying artwork. Bank cards and credit cards have a thin strip of magnetic coating on the back of the cards. Within this strip is information to connect the bank, the bank card holder, and their account all together.

Magnets have invisible magnetic fields that attract certain metals, like iron, steel, and nickel. The earth is a giant magnet, with a North and a South Pole. Magnets can be used in many ways: a compass contains a tiny bar magnet that points toward the earth's North Pole, helping explorers find their way.

2 Mark these measurements on the back of the self-adhesive paper and round off the corners so it matches the corners and size of the cookie sheet. Cut out the self-adhesive paper.

3 Unpeel the paper backing (revealing the sticky side) and stick the self-adhesive paper to the cookie sheet. To help the paper to stick smoothly, unpeel a little at a time as you apply it to the cookie sheet, keeping it as smooth as possible.

4 Your cookie sheet magnet board is ready to use! Lean it against your wall or desk, and start sticking things on with your magnets!

More cookie sheet magnet board ideas:

- *Countdown calendar: use a dry eraser marker and mark off squares for the days of the week. You can count down special days like birthdays, holidays, or days until vacation.*

- *Travel desk: flat and stable, a cookie sheet magnet board is a perfect travel desk to sit on your lap while you are in the car.*

Greeting Card Box

Keep old greeting cards to make these handy boxes.

MAKE IT IN: 15 minutes
BOREDOM BUSTER: One time activity (but keeps forever)
ACTIVITY LEVEL: ★★

Origami meets eco-friendly in this cool craft. With a few simple folds and cuts you can transform an old greeting card into a pretty box. You can then use it as a new gift box or an organizer for your supplies, notes, or bits and pieces.

Things you need:

- Greeting card: this activity works brilliantly with rectangle and square greeting cards but not with oval or round shapes
- Scissors
- Ruler
- Pencil
- Sticky tape

1 On a flat surface, cut the greeting card along the central fold so that you have two pieces the same size.

2 Take the bottom of the card (the part that you write on). Using a ruler and pencil, measure and mark the card with guidelines positioned ¾in (2cm) in from the edge on all four sides.

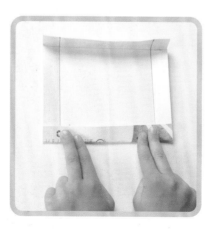

3 Following the pencil guidelines, fold the edge of the card in by ¾in (2cm) on all four sides of the card.

4 With the card facing you, use scissors to cut along the short marked line in the bottom left corner, just to where it meets the corner of the marked square. Do the same thing in the opposite corner of the card, cutting in from the outside along the ¾in (2cm) line to where it meets the corner of the square.

5 Repeat step 4 on the other side of the card. Now fold and crease the square corners toward the inside. Fold and crease the long outside edge, starting with the left edge.

6 Use a piece of sticky tape to secure the edge to the corner square. Do the same thing in all three remaining corners, bringing up the edges of the card and securing the sides together with tape. The bottom of your Greeting Card Box is done!

7 Take the top of the card (the part with the design). Repeat steps 2 to 6 to make the top of the box. Place the top of the Greeting Card Box over the bottom and you are done!

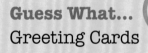

Guess What...
Greeting Cards

People have been sending greetings for thousands of years—the Ancient Egyptians would send messages on papyrus. Handmade cards were common until, in the mid-nineteenth century, mass produced cards became available. There are now cards for every occasion, popular wishes include: Happy Birthday, Thank You, Feel Better, Good Luck, or Well Done.

Microwave Play Dough

Using common household ingredients, you can make your own homemade play dough in no time at all. This dough is just as good as the store-bought stuff and it will provide hours of rolling, shaping, and kneading fun.

MAKE IT IN: **10 minutes**
BOREDOM BUSTER: **One time activity (but you can make it again and again)**
ACTIVITY LEVEL: ★★★

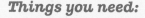

Things you need:

- Microwave-safe bowl with lid (if you don't have a lid you can cover the bowl with plastic wrap/clingfilm)
- 1 cup (120 g) all-purpose (plain) flour
- ⅓ cup (120 g) salt
- 2 tsp cream of tartar
- Spoon
- 1 cup (240 ml) water
- 1 tbsp vegetable oil
- Food coloring (you could also use powdered fruit drink crystals for a scented/colorful play dough)
- Airtight container

1 Measure and pour the flour, salt, and cream of tartar into a microwave-safe bowl. Stir everything together well with a spoon.

2 Mix in the water and oil, add four drops of food coloring, and then stir again.

Guess What... Cream of Tartar

Cream of tartar is a white, crystal powder. It comes from countries where wine is made. The crystals are formed naturally in wine barrels after grape juice has fermented into wine. Cream of tartar has no smell and tastes acidic. It is an ingredient in baking powder.

Stop for safety!

Ask an adult to help you to use the microwave.

Read the directions carefully and measure well (too little or too much of something can ruin the dough).

DO NOT EAT Microwave Play Dough (it is not food).

3 Put the lid on the bowl (or cover with plastic wrap/clingfilm) and ask an adult to help you to microwave on high for 2 minutes.

4 Carefully take the bowl out of the microwave, and then, carefully again, take the lid or plastic wrap/clingfilm off the bowl, avoiding any hot steam which might escape. Stir with a spoon. Put the lid or plastic wrap back on the bowl and return it to the microwave for another 30 seconds on high. If the play dough is still sticky, microwave it again for another 30 seconds. Let it cool.

5 Knead and play! What does the play dough feel like? Is it hard? Soft? Wet? Dry? When you're done playing, store the play dough in an airtight container. To help clean up the bowl, soak it in water for a while before cleaning.

More microwave play dough ideas:

Make shapes (circles, squares, triangles, hearts); animals (dog, caterpillar, elephant, snake); letters and numbers (ABC, 123); objects (snowman, car, house, blocks, happy face); and pretend play (pretend you are cooking, cutting, and serving foods like pizza, apples, pasta).

Duct Tape Crayon Holder

Never misplace your crayons again! This Duct Tape Crayon Holder is fun to make and super useful in any art project. Bonus: it is compact too, making it small enough to roll up and easily store in your art area, school bag, or suitcase so you can have an art attack whenever the mood hits you.

MAKE IT IN: **30 minutes**
BOREDOM BUSTER: **One time activity (but keeps forever)**
ACTIVITY LEVEL: ★ ★ ★

Things you need:

• 2 rolls of large duct tape in different colors
• Ruler
• Scissors
• 6 crayons
• Ribbon, string, or shoelace, about 18in (46cm) long

1 Cut three strips of duct tape, each 7in (18cm) long. Place each strip sticky side up on your activity surface so that they won't stick to the table.

2 Overlap the strips lengthwise, sticky side up, so that they stick together making a rectangle.

3 Using your second color of duct tape, repeat steps 1 and 2. Now place the two rectangles sticky sides together, so that they stick together to make a piece of fabric.

4 Trim the duct tape rectangle with your scissors to cut off any rough or uneven edges.

Duct tape is available in a variety of colors and patterns!

5 To make the crayon pockets, take your second color of duct tape and cut one piece 7in (18cm) long. Then cut six smaller, narrow strips about 1in (2.5cm) each across the width.

6 Place each of the six strips, sticky side down, onto the sticky side of the long piece of duct tape, leaving a small space between each of the six strips (at each end and in between) because these gaps need to stick to your rectangle fabric.

Duct tape is water-resistant, so if you happen to spill your water bottle on the crayon roll, it will easily wipe dry.

7 Stick the crayon pocket strip onto the inside of the crayon roll, along the bottom edge, so that the long edges of the strip and roll are lined up. For a smooth bottom edge, fold the pocket strip to the outside, if you like. Trim any rough edges.

8 Insert your crayons into the pockets: it will hold six crayons.

9 Cut a small piece of the first color of duct tape. Fold the piece of ribbon, string, or shoelace in half and attach the folded end to the small piece of duct tape. Attach the tape and ribbon to the outside edge of the crayon roll. Position it so that is attached about halfway down one short edge and so that the long ends of the ribbon face out, away from the roll.

10 Roll up crayon duct tape roll, wrap the ribbon around it a few times, and tie the ends in a bow.

Guess What...
Sticky Stuff

Duct tape sometimes leaves a gummy residue on your scissors (yuck!). To remove duct tape residue from your scissor blades just use ordinary rubbing alcohol. Take a tissue or cotton ball, dab it in a bit of rubbing alcohol, and carefully clean your blades. When the gunk is gone, rinse the scissors in warm water and then wipe dry with a clean tissue or cotton ball. Wash your hands after cleaning scissors (rubbing alcohol can dry your skin).

CHAPTER 3
Science Activities

Goo-tastic!

Call it goo, slime, gak, flubber, or crazy putty, this activity is fantastic! You could even say it's goo-tastic! However, you have to follow the directions perfectly for it to work. So read all of the step-by-step information before you start. Then, while you are doing it, read the directions aloud to yourself, making sure you follow all of the steps.

MAKE IT IN: **15 minutes**
BOREDOM BUSTER: **Over and over again**
ACTIVITY LEVEL: ★ ★ ★

Things you need:

- Activity mat or old newspaper
- Apron
- 2 containers: re-use clean yogurt containers or use medium-sized bowls
- Mixing spoons
- Measuring cup and spoons
- ½ cup (120 ml) warm water
- Borax laundry detergent
- ¼ cup (60 ml) school glue (white PVA glue)
- Food coloring

1 Protect your activity surface by putting down an activity mat or some newspaper. Wash your hands, roll up your sleeves, and put on an apron to protect your clothes.

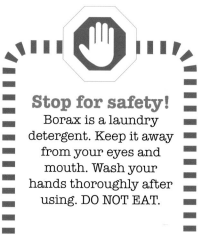

Stop for safety!
Borax is a laundry detergent. Keep it away from your eyes and mouth. Wash your hands thoroughly after using. DO NOT EAT.

2 Pour half the warm water (¼ cup/60 ml) into one container and add ½ teaspoon of borax. Stir with your measuring spoon to dissolve all the borax. Set this container aside.

3 Put the second container on the activity mat. Measure out ¼ cup (60 ml) of white PVA glue. Keep stirring the glue while you slowly add the remaining ¼ cup (60 ml) of warm water to thin out the glue.

4 Now add four drops of food coloring to the diluted glue and stir it in.

5 Take your first container (with the borax mixture) and give it a good stir.

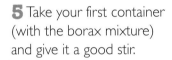

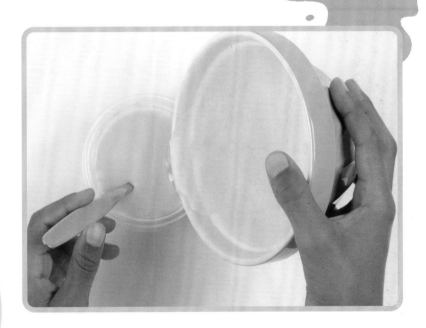

Goo will keep in an airtight container for approximately three weeks. After that, throw it in the garbage (NOT down the sink—it will block the pipes!). Then make another batch.

6 VERY IMPORTANT STEP! Slowly (very, very slowly) drip the borax mixture (in the first container) into the glue (in the second container) while constantly stirring with a spoon. If you pour in the borax mixture all at once, it will ruin the goo. For slimier goo, add half of the borax mixture; for firmer goo, add all of the borax mixture.

Guess What... White Glue

White glue (also called school or PVA glue) sticks because as it dries, water is evaporated from the chemicals in the glue, changing its molecular structure. As the water evaporates, the molecules in the glue change from liquid to solid, making it sticky.

7 At first, it will look like a watery mess—that's OK! When the goo starts sticking to the spoon, take the goo out of the container and work it with your hands, pressing and stretching it. The goo will be super runny and slimy when you start working with it but the more you press it, the firmer it will get.

8 If you put the goo on your activity mat it will relax and look like a liquid. However, if you knead the goo in your hands, it will start to feel like a sort of soft rubber. What do YOU think? Is goo a liquid or a solid? Does it feel soft or hard? Does it stretch or break?

Caution: goo will be ruined if it gets wet.

Magic Milk

Want to make a rainbow in your kitchen? YES PLEASE! Magic milk is a quick activity that creates a moving color wheel in a bowl. Never the same result twice, you will want to do this activity over and over again!

MAKE IT IN: **2 minutes**
BOREDOM BUSTER: **One time rainbow (but you can do it again and again)**
ACTIVITY LEVEL: ★

Things you need:

- ½ cup (115 ml) milk
- A large flat bowl, like a soup bowl
- Food coloring in different colors
- Q-tips (cotton buds)
- Dishwashing detergent

1 Pour the milk into the bowl and add a few drops of food coloring in different colors in the middle of the milk.

2 Dip the end of a Q-tip (cotton bud) in a little dishwashing detergent. Now, dip this Q-tip into the center of the food coloring—don't swirl or stir the Q-tip, just dip it and hold it in the center of the bowl.

3 Are the colors staying in one place or moving around? What happens if the colors touch? Does the color wheel ever stop?

The science

The dishwashing detergent on the Q-tip (cotton bud) changes the surface tension in the milk, allowing the colors to swirl around. Re-do it with different colors and see what happens. Surface tension is when the milk molecules on the surface hold onto each other tightly so that a "skin" forms. The detergent weakens the links in the molecules and the dye has a chance to move around, swirling between them.

Guess What... Milk

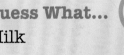

Milk comes from many mammals including cows, sheep, and goats. However, milk can also be produced from soybeans, coconut, rice, and almonds.

Pepper on the Run

This is a quick activity for a rainy day or as an after-school Boredom Buster. Have you ever seen pepper run? How can something run if it doesn't have feet?! Pepper on the Run is an easy science experiment that explores how things move.

MAKE IT IN: **2 minutes**
BOREDOM BUSTER: **One
    time activity (but you
    can do it again and
    again)**
ACTIVITY LEVEL: ★

• • • • • • • • • • • • • • • • • • •

Things you need:

- ⅛ cup (115 ml) milk
- A large flat bowl, like a soup bowl
- A dash of ground pepper
- A dab of dishwashing detergent

1 Pour the milk into the bowl. Sprinkle a dash of pepper onto the milk. Watch how the pepper floats on top of the milk.

Guess What... Pepper

The pepper plant is grown in tropical countries like India and Vietnam. The dried fruit of the pepper plant is called a peppercorn. When peppercorns are ground up we call it black pepper. Pepper is the world's most traded spice and is used to season food to give it a slightly hot, spicy taste.

2 Next, put a dab of dishwashing detergent on your fingertip.

3 Put your finger in the milk. What happens to the pepper? Is the pepper "running" or staying in one place? If you repeat the activity, does exactly the same thing happen again or is there a different result?

The science

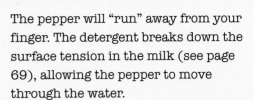

The pepper will "run" away from your finger. The detergent breaks down the surface tension in the milk (see page 69), allowing the pepper to move through the water.

Plastic Bottle Tornados

Reuse a couple of plastic bottles from the recycling for this great project.

MAKE IT IN: **15 minutes**
BOREDOM BUSTER: **Makes one (but you can play with it over and over)**
ACTIVITY LEVEL: ★ ★ ★

Don't throw away that plastic bottle! This is a great opportunity for an activity that is science, weather, and eco-friendly experiment all rolled into one! Make sure you use two of the same-sized plastic bottles.

Things you need:

- Activity mat or old newspaper
- 2 clear (and clean) plastic bottles, both the same size
- Water
- Food coloring or glitter (optional)
- Scissors
- Plastic wrap (clingfilm)
- Duct tape

Stop for safety!
Ask an adult to supervize cutting the duct tape.

1 Protect your activity surface by putting down an activity mat or some old newspaper—spills happen! Peel the labels off the plastic bottles and remove the caps (you don't need them again but you could use them for another art activity).

2 Fill one of the bottles three-quarters full with water. If you like, add a few drops of food coloring or a sprinkle of glitter to the water.

Guess What...
Tornados

Tornados are strong, spinning air columns touching both the clouds and the ground. Tornado winds are extremely powerful and can create massive damage and destruction. Tornado winds have measured up to 500 km (300 miles) per hour. They are also called twisters.

3 Cut a strip of plastic wrap (clingfilm), long enough to go around the bottle tops. Next, cut three strips of duct tape about the same length as the plastic wrap strip.

4 Pick up the empty plastic bottle, turn it upside down, and connect it to the bottle that is filled with water—with their necks joining. Wrap the plastic wrap very, very tightly around the plastic bottle necks, connecting them together (this is your water seal so that the liquid doesn't spill out).

5 Wrap the duct tape around the plastic wrap from the top of the plastic wrap to the bottom. Wrap it tightly to stabilize the two bottles (they should be firmly connected).

6 Turn the bottles over to check that the water doesn't drip out. If it does, it means the plastic wrap wasn't tight enough, so take off the duct tape and re-do steps 4 and 5.

7 Swoosh the water-filled-bottle in a circular motion to get the water moving around and then turn it upside down. Watch for a mini tornado in the water-filled-bottle.

8 What do you see happening? Is the water moving quickly or slowly? Why do you think that is?

Homemade Bubbles

Bubbles are a great outside activity. Blow, pop, float, drop—bubbles are fantastic. Did you know you have everything to make your very own Homemade Bubbles in your kitchen?! Easy and inexpensive—this activity is tons of outdoor fun!

MAKE IT IN: **5 minutes**
BOREDOM BUSTER: **One time activity (but can make it again and again)**
ACTIVITY LEVEL: ★

Things you need:

- ½ cup (115 ml) dishwashing detergent
- 1¼ cups (340 ml) water
- 2 tsp granulated sugar
- Bowl
- Measuring cup
- Spoon
- Pipe cleaner or string

This is an **OUTSIDE** activity

1 Measure out the dishwashing detergent, water, and sugar into a bowl and stir together.

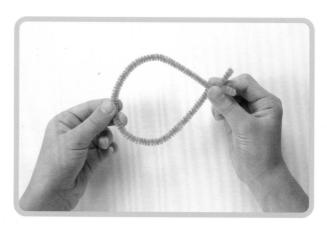

2 Now all you need is a bubble wand! To make your own bubble wand, twist the end of a pipe cleaner round to make a circle about 1½in (4cm) in diameter, then keep twisting the ends to make a straight end that you can hold as a "wand."

The science

When you watch bubbles float you see which way the wind is blowing. If the wind is blowing south...the bubbles will float south. If the wind is blowing east... the bubbles will float east.

3 To make a string wand, take a piece of string about 8in (20cm) long and knot the ends together to make a circle.

4 Take your bowl of bubble liquid outside. If you are using a string wand, insert your two pointer fingers and two thumbs on each side to hold the circle taut and dip it in the bubble solution. With your fingers in place, take the string out of the bubble solution and gently blow through the circle—bubbles!

5 Whether your bubble wand is made of string, pipe cleaner, or wire, continue to dip it into the mixture, and gently blow through the ring. Do the bubbles float up or do they crash down? What happens if one bubble touches another bubble?

Guess What...
Bubbles

When we think of bubbles we usually think of circle-shaped, floating, flying, popping bubbles made out of soap and water. But guess what, there is an animal with bubble properties. Bubble Eye Goldfish have water filled bubble sacks on each side of their faces. If one of their bubble sacks pops it will re-grow!

Grow Your Own Crystals

Ever wanted to grow your own crystals? Now you can—and the bonus is you do it indoors! Grow Your Own Crystals look so nice they are perfect window decorations to keep for yourself or to give as gifts. This activity works better the longer you leave it, so it's recommended to do it as a week-long project.

MAKE IT IN: **24 hours to 1 week**

BOREDOM BUSTER: **One time activity (but keeps for months)**

ACTIVITY LEVEL: ★ ★ ★

Things you need:

- Pipe cleaner
- String
- Scissors
- Wide kilner (mason) jar or a wide preserve jar
- Pencil
- Measuring cup
- Food coloring
- Spoon
- Borax laundry detergent

1 Start by asking an adult to help you to boil water in the kettle.

2 Twist the pipe cleaner into a shape—a heart, flower, shamrock, candy cane, circle, star, or whatever shape you like.

3 Cut a piece of string a little longer than the height of the jar. Tie one end of the string to your pipe cleaner and the other end to the pencil.

4 Ask an adult to help you measure out one cup (230 ml) of boiling water and pour it into the jar—pour slowly and carefully. Drip four drops of food coloring into the water in the jar.

5 Add three tablespoons of borax to the jar and stir well with a spoon.

6 Gently lower your pipe cleaner into the jar, balancing the pencil on the top of the jar, so that the pipe cleaner hangs inside the borax mixture. IMPORTANT: The pipe cleaner shape should not touch the bottom or sides of the jar. If it does, untie the knot on the pencil and re-tie it so that the pipe cleaner hangs free.

7 Leave the jar to sit overnight (or for a week) somewhere where it won't be disturbed or moved, and away from sunlight or heat. Watch and wait as the crystals begin to grow. You will start seeing crystals form within 24 hours but if you wait a week, the crystals will completely cover the shape. These crystal decorations last for months.

8 Do the crystals grow in one place or do they cover the shape? Are there big and small crystals or do they all look about the same size?

Guess What...
Crystals

The word crystal comes from the Greek word "krustallos," which means both ice and crystal. Scientists who study "crystallography" study crystals. There are many different types of crystals, such as sugar, salt, rock, snow, and ice.

Effervescent Rockets

"Effervescent" is a weird word, right? Say it like this: effer-ves-cent. It means: bubbling. This activity uses a tablet that makes bubbles, with explosive results! You must do this activity outside—in the back yard, on a lawn, or at the park—not in your living room or kitchen as the rockets can pop pretty high!

MAKE IT IN: **2 minutes**
BOREDOM BUSTER: **One time activity (but you can make as many rockets as you have tablets)**
ACTIVITY LEVEL: ★★

1 Before you send your rocket into the stratosphere, you could decorate it to make it look like a real rocket. Use marker pens and/or stickers to make flames and portholes for your rocket.

Things you need:

- Small plastic canisters with a snap-on lid, like film canisters, medicine, or vitamin canisters (this activity will not work with a screw-on lid canister)
- Marker pens (like Sharpies) and/or stickers (optional)
- Packet of effervescent tablets, like Alka-Seltzer—ask an adult to help you find them
- Water

2 Go outside. Put the canister (the rocket) on a flat surface: a patio, path, or driveway is nice and flat!

This is an **OUTSIDE** activity

Stop for safety!
Effervescent tablets are generally medications. They are found at the pharmacy and/or in your medicine cabinet. Ask an adult to help you find the correct tablet to use. DO NOT EAT IT.

As the effervescent tablet and water combine together inside the canister they create gas. As the gas pressure builds it blows the snap-on lid and canister upward.

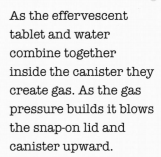

3 Break an effervescent tablet in half. Fill the canister one-third full with water. Add half the tablet to the canister.

4 Quickly put the lid on the canister. STAND BACK! The rocket may take a few seconds to pop so do not go back to check on it. Certainly do not stand over it (it could blow anytime and you don't want to get hit in the eye with your rocket). Stand back and watch. It's pretty neat.

5 What do you see? Does it pop straight away or does it take time to blow up? Is there a noise? Measure how far the lid travels from the canister.

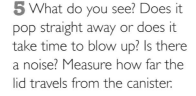

Guess What... Alka-Seltzer

Alka-Seltzer is a an effervescent tablet medication that helps relieve pain (there are different kinds—some for headaches, some for upset tummy, some for colds). The main ingredient in Alka-Seltzer is sodium bicarbonate (baking soda). Alka-Seltzer fizzes because of a chemical reaction of ingredients in the tablet—when combined with water, they produce gas.

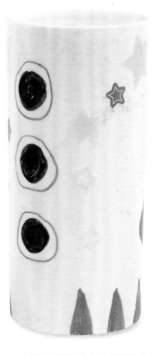

Lava in a Cup

Lava is, generally, something that bubbles out of a volcano. However, in this easy activity you can make your own, bubbling Lava in a Cup, using things you already have in your kitchen cabinet—creating a neat science experiment. If you want to repeat the Lava in a Cup activity, you have to use a clean glass with new ingredients each time.

MAKE IT IN: **2 minutes**
BOREDOM BUSTER: **One time activity (but you can do it again and again)**
ACTIVITY LEVEL: ★

Things you need:

- A clear drinking glass
- ¾ cup (170 ml) water
- Food coloring
- ¼ cup (60 ml) vegetable oil
- 1 tsp salt

1 Pour the water into the glass, then add five drops of food coloring to the water.

2 Now add the vegetable oil to the glass.

3 Finally, add the teaspoon of salt into the mixture.

4 What do you notice? Does the lava move up or down? Does the lava ever move left or right?

The science

Oil is lighter than water so it will sit on top of the water. Salt is heavier than water so it will fall—taking some vegetable oil down with it to make "lava."

Guess What... Food Coloring

You can make food coloring in your kitchen by boiling certain fruits and vegetables, with water, in a pan on your stove. Boiling the fruits and veggies draws out the natural color into the water. Remember to boil just one fruit or one vegetable at a time to get the desired color, and to ask an adult to help you with the hot pan. Add 2 cups (500 ml) of water to a saucepan. Put in your vegetable, cover with a lid, and bring to a boil. Simmer for 15 minutes, turn off the heat, and let cool to room temperature. Throw the veggies away (don't eat them, all of the goodness has gone into the water). You can fish the veggies out or place a bowl under a strainer and strain the colored water.
- Beets (beetroot) = pink dye
- Blueberries = blue dye
- Spinach = green dye
- Carrots = yellow dye

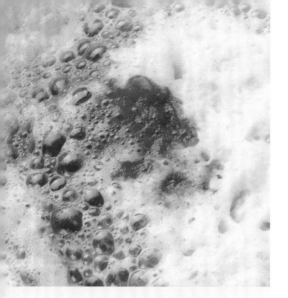

Rainbow-cano

It's a rainbow. It's a volcano. It's a Rainbow-cano! This easy homemade volcano can be created in no time at all and provides tons of fun. What's different about this volcano is the use of food coloring to create a rainbow eruption. A Rainbow-cano can be messy, so be sure to protect your activity surface!

MAKE IT IN: **5 minutes**
BOREDOM BUSTER: **One time activity (but you can make it again and again)**
ACTIVITY LEVEL: ★★

Things you need:

- Activity mat or old newspaper
- Apron or old T-shirt
- Cookie (baking) sheet
- Medium-sized bowl
- 2 tbsp baking soda
- Food coloring in at least 3 different colors
- Measuring cup
- ¼ cup (60 ml) vinegar

1 Protect your activity surface by putting down an activity mat or some newspaper. Tie up your hair, roll up your sleeves, and put on an apron or old T-shirt to protect your clothes. Put the cookie (baking) sheet on your work surface (this will catch the lava if it spills out of the bowl).

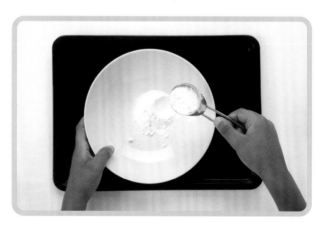

2 Place the bowl on top of the cookie sheet and add the baking soda to the bowl.

The science

When baking soda and vinegar are combined they create a fizzing reaction, producing bubbles and a lava-like oozing effect. You can also try this activity without the food coloring to see what happens when there is no color.

3 On one side of the baking soda, drop two drops of food coloring. On the opposite side drop two drops of a different color of food coloring and then add two more drops of a different color at the top.

4 Slowly pour the vinegar into the bowl on top of the baking soda. Watch and wait!

5 Do the colors stay on their own sides or do they blend together? What does it smell like? Does the activity work right away or do you have to wait to see a result?

Guess What...
Baking Soda

Baking soda can be used in so many places:

- In the kitchen for baking (it makes cakes rise)
- In the nursery (it cleans baby toys)
- In the bathroom (it gets rid of dirt)
- In the laundry room (it gets rid of stains)
- In your school bag (it gets rid of forgotten lunch smells)

Indoor Sprouts

What is a "sprout" you ask? A sprout is a small plant growing out from a seed. Grow your very own indoor garden using this simple science. Keep your sprouts near a window so that they can get all the goodness they need (from the sun) to grow.

MAKE IT IN: **1 week**
BOREDOM BUSTER: **One time activity**
ACTIVITY LEVEL: ★

Things you need:

• Paper (kitchen) towel
• Water
• A shallow container or bowl: a clean margarine tub or plastic fruit carton will do
• ¼ cup (60 g) dry lentils

1 Moisten the paper (kitchen) towel with water (but not so it is soaking wet) and use it to line the bottom of your shallow container.

2 Sprinkle the dry lentils evenly over the moistened paper towel.

3 Cover the lentils with another sheet of moist paper towel.

Guess What...

Sprouts

Sprouts are a healthy source of fiber. You can grow other sprouts at home, too. Try some of these: alfalfa sprouts, lentils, cress, chickpeas, soybeans, and peas. Sprouts are a great addition to a sandwich or salad.

4 Put your container near a window with full sunlight. Every day add a little bit of water to ensure that the paper towel remains moist (try not to soak it!). Do not uncover the paper towel to check on the sprouts. They will find their own way out of the paper towel. Just watch.

5 Within a week you will see your sprouts sprout! You can use scissors to give your sprouts a haircut, if you like.

6 What do you see happening? Do you see sprouts finding their way to the sunlight? What does a plant need in order to grow?

Homemade Snow

Have you ever wished you could play with snow indoors?! Homemade snow is actually cool to the touch and packable so you can make mini snowballs or snow men, just like the real thing! Homemade snow will smell lovely but please DO NOT EAT it!

MAKE IT IN: **5 minutes**
BOREDOM BUSTER: **Over and over again**
ACTIVITY LEVEL: ★

Things you need:

- Activity mat or old newspaper
- Apron or old T-shirt
- Large container or dish (a lasagne pan or big plastic container work well!)
- 1½ cups (340 g) baking soda
- ¼ cup (115 ml) hair conditioner
- Measuring cups
- Spoon
- Cups to dig and fill (optional)

1 Protect your activity surface by putting down an activity mat or some newspaper. Tie up your hair, roll up your sleeves, and put on an apron or old T-shirt to protect your clothes. Make sure the activity mat is on a flat surface (to catch any snow that might "spill" out). You can do this activity on the floor or on a table.

2 Place a large container on the activity mat and measure out the baking soda into the container. Now add the hair conditioner: white conditioner will make white snow; pink conditioner will make pink snow.

Other homemade snow ideas:

Having a winter-themed birthday party? You could hide some small gemstones at the bottom of a container, cover them with this homemade snow, and have your guests dig in the snow to uncover the treasures.

3 Use a spoon to mix together the hair conditioner with the baking soda. Your snow is ready! What does this snow feel like? Is it grainy? Soft? Hard? Dry? Wet?

Do not eat homemade snow!

Guess What...
Snow

If you live in a cold region, snow is part of your winter outdoor life. There are lots of snow-inspired activities:
- skiing
- sledding
- snowboarding
- snowmobiling
- dog sledding
- snow shoeing
- bobsledding
- ski jumping
- igloo building

CHAPTER 4
Food Activities

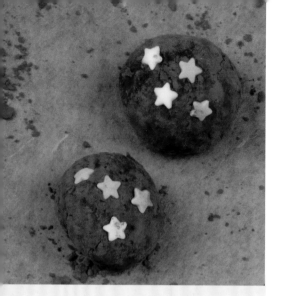

Melt in Your Mouth Chocolate Treats

This is a great no-bake, no-cook dessert. Crumble, pat, roll, and dip—this activity uses lots of hand movements to make these yummy treats. Make this activity for your next celebration party because these Melt in Your Mouth Chocolate Treats are extraordinarily delicious!

MAKE IT IN: **45 minutes**
BOREDOM BUSTER: **One time activity**
ACTIVITY LEVEL: ★ ★

Things you need:

- Apron
- Chocolate cake: homemade or store-bought, such as a pound cake or a 9in (23cm) cake
- Large and small bowls
- Fork and spoon
- 4-8 oz (115-225 g) chocolate frosting (icing), which is ¼ to ½ of an average container, depending on how sweet you like your treats
- Airtight container with a lid
- ½ cup (60 g) cocoa powder
- Cookie or baking sheet, lined with baking parchment paper
- Sugar sprinkles

Makes about 25

1 Wash your hands, roll up your sleeves, and put on an apron to protect your clothes. Using your fingers, break the cake into pieces and put them in a bowl.

2 Using a fork, crumble the cake until it is all broken up and looks like sand.

3 Spoon a quarter of the chocolate frosting (icing) into the crumbled cake and mix together using the spoon.

4 Spoon the cake/frosting mixture into an airtight container and chill in the fridge for 15 minutes (or leave the mixture in the fridge overnight).

5 When chilled, take the cake/frosting mixture from the fridge. Using your hands (wash them again first, please!), roll the cake mixture into small balls (about the size of a ping pong ball).

6 Put the cocoa powder in a small bowl and roll the chocolate balls in the powder to cover them. Place the finished chocolate balls on the lined cookie sheet.

Guess What...
Chocolate

Chocolate comes from the seeds of the cacao tree. The seeds are roasted, the shells are removed, and the cacao nibs are ground into pure chocolate. By adding sugar and other ingredients we get many types of chocolate: bitter, semi-sweet, white, dark, and milk.

7 If you like, you can decorate the balls with sugar sprinkles. Wash and dry the airtight container then fill it with the cocoa covered chocolate balls. Use parchment paper between the layers. Replace the lid and return the container to the fridge until ready to serve.

These are best eaten the day they are made but will keep for a few days in the fridge.

Yogurt Container Cupcakes

MAKE IT IN: **45 minutes**

BOREDOM BUSTER: **One time activity (but you can make them again and again)**

ACTIVITY LEVEL: ★ ★

Things you need:

- 1 small and 1 large bowl
- 1 single serving container vanilla yogurt (about ½ cup/ 100 ml)
- 1 tsp baking soda
- Spoon
- 1 container vegetable oil
- 1 container white sugar
- 4 containers all-purpose (plain) flour
- 2 eggs
- 1 container milk
- 12-hole cupcake pan, greased or lined with cupcake cases
- Cooling rack
- Frosting (icing) and sprinkles, to decorate (optional)

Makes 12 cupcakes

Individual yogurt containers are terrific for measuring ingredients when you are baking. These scrumptious Yogurt Container Cupcakes make for an excellent afterschool snack, birthday party treat, or even for a grab-and-go weekday breakfast.

1 Ask an adult to help you to turn the oven on to 350°F (180°C/Gas 4) to preheat.

Stop for safety!
Ask an adult to help you with the hot oven.

2 In a small bowl, mix together the vanilla yogurt and baking soda—watch it double in size!

3 Next, wash and dry the yogurt container and use it as your measuring cup for the rest of the ingredients. In a large bowl combine the oil and sugar and mix them together well.

4 Add the flour, eggs, and milk to the large bowl and mix again.

5 Take the small bowl with the yogurt and baking soda mixture, and add it to the large bowl. Now mix everything together until the batter is smooth.

Guess What...
Yogurt

Yogurt is a popular dairy product eaten all over the world. It can be made from the milk of cows, sheep, or goats. Yogurt is an excellent source of energy. It can come in many varieties such as: low-fat, Greek-style, fruit layered, stirred, drinkable, and frozen.

Yogurt can be spelled in three different ways: yogurt, yoghurt, and yoghourt.

More cupcake ideas:

You can change this recipe by adding a container of frozen blueberries, raspberries, or strawberry slices to the mixture in step 5. You could also try this same recipe using different flavors of yogurt.

6 Pour the batter into a greased cupcake pan or into cupcake cases in a cupcake pan, and bake in the oven for 15–22 minutes, until the cupcakes are risen and golden.

7 Ask an adult to help you remove the pan from the oven and let cool on a wire rack. Enjoy your cupcakes as they are, or decorate them with frosting (icing), sprinkles, or even Invisible Icing (see opposite).

You can use this recipe to make the Ice Cream Cone Cupcakes (see page 100), too!

Invisible Icing

Created for a kid who didn't like frosting on her cupcakes... invisible icing is easy to make for children of all ages. There are just two simple ingredients (which you probably already have in your kitchen) to make this sweet treat.

MAKE IT IN: **5 minutes**
BOREDOM BUSTER: **One time activity (but you can make it again and again)**
ACTIVITY LEVEL: ★

Things you need:

- Confectioner's (icing) sugar
- Measuring spoon
- Medium-sized bowl
- Water
- Sugar sprinkles (optional)

1 Measure out five teaspoons of confectioner's (icing) sugar into the bowl.

2 Carefully add three or four drops of water and mix together well. The frosting will look quite runny—but that's OK!

3 Drizzle the icing over the cupcakes and then decorate with sprinkles, if you like.

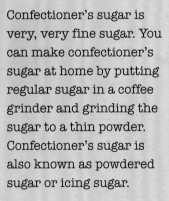

Guess What...
Confectioner's Sugar

Confectioner's sugar is very, very fine sugar. You can make confectioner's sugar at home by putting regular sugar in a coffee grinder and grinding the sugar to a thin powder. Confectioner's sugar is also known as powdered sugar or icing sugar.

Microwave Granola

Microwave Granola is healthy, simple to make, and a great go-to snack when you get the munchies. It's also easy to adapt the recipe by adding other ingredients (see box below). Cut the granola into triangles and eat them whole as a snack, or crumble the granola and sprinkle it onto your breakfast yogurt.

MAKE IT IN: **10 minutes**
BOREDOM BUSTER: **One time activity (but you can make it again and again)**
ACTIVITY LEVEL: ★ ★

Things you need:

- Glass pie plate
- Cooking spray
- Bowl
- Spoon
- 2 cups (160 g) quick-cook porridge oats (rolled oats)
- 1 tsp flour
- 1 tsp ground flax seed (source of fiber!)
- 5 tbsp (80 g) butter, softened
- ⅓ cup (80 ml) maple syrup
- 1 egg, beaten
- Measuring cup (jug)
- ⅓ cup (50 g) raisins
- ⅓ cup (50 g) mini chocolate chips

Makes 6 triangles

1 Spray the glass pie plate with cooking spray—this will make cleaning up easier!

2 Pour the oats, flour, and flax seed into the bowl and mix together.

3 Mix the butter, maple syrup, and beaten egg in a measuring cup (jug) and pour it over the oat mixture, then mix everything together well.

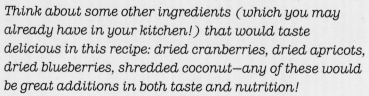

More granola ideas:

Think about some other ingredients (which you may already have in your kitchen!) that would taste delicious in this recipe: dried cranberries, dried apricots, dried blueberries, shredded coconut—any of these would be great additions in both taste and nutrition!

4 Next, add the raisins and chocolate chips. Stir them in well.

5 Pour the granola mix into the pie plate and flatten it with the back of a spoon.

6 Ask an adult to help you to microwave the pie plate for 5 minutes on high.

7 Carefully take the plate out of the microwave. Use a blunt knife to mark out squares or triangles and set aside to let cool. Cut into triangles or squares following your marks.

Fingertip Fudge

Fingertip Fudge is always a hit. It might be the hands-on fun of smooshing the fudge with your fingers. It could be squeezing the fudge out of the bag. Or it could be the deliciousness of licking the fudge itself. You will LOVE making this recipe! To make a smaller batch, simply halve each of the ingredients.

MAKE IT IN: **5 minutes**
BOREDOM BUSTER: **One time activity (but you can make it again and again)**
ACTIVITY LEVEL: ★

Things you need:

- Large bowl
- ½ cup (120 g) cream cheese
- ½ cup (60 g) cocoa powder
- 2 tbsp (30 g) softened butter
- 2 cups (250 g) confectioner's (icing) sugar
- 1 large re-sealable plastic bag
- Scissors

Makes about 10 servings

This fudge is a great frosting alternative for Ice Cream Cone Cupcakes (see page 100).

1 In a large bowl, combine the cream cheese, cocoa powder, and softened butter. Mix them together well.

2 Add a tablespoon of confectioner's (icing) sugar and mix it in. Continue adding the sugar a tablespoon at a time (you don't want to pour all the sugar in at once because it will be hard to stir).

3 Once the ingredients are all combined, spoon the mixture into the re-sealable plastic bag. Seal tight. You can divide up the mixture into small re-sealable plastic bags if you want to share the activity with your friends.

4 Then the fun begins! Smoosh and squish the fudge-in-a-bag as much as you like using your fingertips, hands, and even armpits!

5 Cut a hole in the corner of the plastic bag and squeeze out the fudge. Enjoy! If you like, you could use the fudge to frost (ice) either store-bought or homemade cupcakes.

Guess What...
Cream Cheese

Cream cheese is made of milk. It has a very mild creamy taste and is white in color. Cream cheese can be spread on toast or bagels, baked in cakes, or combined with herbs to make a dip.

Ice Cream Cone Cupcakes

This is a treat to WOW your party guests—bake cupcakes in ice cream cones! Not only are these cupcakes a really unique way to present dessert, they are also super easy to make. The ice cream cones start going soft after about a day, so plan on making-and-taking them within 24 hours.

MAKE IT IN: **45 minutes**
BOREDOM BUSTER: **One time activity (but you can make them again and again)**
ACTIVITY LEVEL: ★

Things you need:

- Medium bowl
- Wooden spoon or electric mixer
- 1 packet of cake mix or use the **Yogurt Container Cupcake** recipe on page 92
- 12 regular flat-bottom ice cream cones
- 12-hole cupcake pan
- Frosting, or use the **Fingertip Fudge** recipe on page 98
- Cardboard cereal box and scissors (optional)

Makes 12 cupcakes

More ideas:

To make an Ice Cream Cone Cupcake carrier, re-use an empty cardboard cereal box! With the supervision of an adult, cut away one side of the box and then score 12 "X"s in the bottom. Place an ice cream cone cupcake in each X.

1 Ask an adult to help you to turn the oven on to 350°F (180°C/Gas 4) to preheat.

Stop for safety!
Ask an adult to help you with the hot oven.

2 Prepare the cake mix as directed on the packet, or make the Yogurt Container Cupcake batter following the instructions on page 92.

3 In a cupcake pan, line up 12 flat-bottom ice cream cones.

4 Spoon the cake batter into each ice cream cone until it is just over halfway full. As with regular cupcakes, these cupcakes will rise as they bake. This is why you don't want to fill the cones to the top because then they may rise and spill over the sides of the ice cream cone.

5 Ask an adult to help you to put the cupcake pan in the oven, carefully so that the cones don't fall over. Bake for 15–22 minutes, or until the cakes are risen and golden. You can use the Fingertip Fudge to decorate the cakes, if you like.

Guess What...
Ice Cream Cones

Before ice cream cones were invented, people ate ice cream out of small glasses called "Penny Licks." Ice cream vendors would fill a small glass (the "penny lick") with ice cream for a penny. The customer would lick out the ice cream and then give the glass back to the vendor to clean and re-use for another customer. Not all vendors cleaned the cups (yuck!) and because of concerns about hygiene, a pastry cup was invented in New York in 1896, which quickly became the popular waffle cone that we still use today.

Sunrise in a Cup

Watch as the colors spread through your glass—just like a sunrise! This layered drink is delicious and a great addition to any birthday party (or breakfast table!). You need to use a clear glass to get the full effect of orange layered over red in this recipe.

MAKE IT IN: **5 minutes**
BOREDOM BUSTER: **One time activity**
ACTIVITY LEVEL: ★

Things you need:

- A tall, clear glass
- ½ cup (125 ml) orange juice
- Spoon
- ¼ cup (60 ml) grenadine syrup (found in the drink aisle of your supermarket)
- Drinking straws (optional)

Makes 1 drink

1 Measure out then pour the orange juice into the clear glass.

Guess What... Grenadine

Grenadine comes from the French word "grenade," which means pomegranate. A pomegranate is a round fruit with a thick outside skin. Inside are hundreds of pomegranate seeds that you eat raw. Pomegranate juice was originally used to make grenadine syrup, giving it the special red color.

Sunset in a Cup:

If you're not a fan of grenadine, why not try this delicious alternative? Replace the grenadine with cranberry juice—the colors will blend together, and still taste great!

2 Take the spoon and hold it over the glass so that the rounded underside is facing up. SLOWLY pour the grenadine syrup over the back of the spoon.

3 The grenadine syrup will sink to the bottom creating a layer of red under the orange juice. Pop a straw in your glass, if you like, and sip away!

Homemade Ice Cream

This is an awesome activity to do during your next school vacation. Homemade Ice Cream is half food activity and half science activity! Oh, and pretty delicious too! The key to making Homemade Ice Cream is to ensure the re-sealable bags are completely closed. If one is a little open you could end up with very salty ice cream (yuck!).

MAKE IT IN: **15 minutes**
BOREDOM BUSTER: **One time activity (but you can make it again and again)**
ACTIVITY LEVEL: ★ ★

Things you need:

- 2 re-sealable plastic bags (1 large and 1 small)
- 12 ice cubes
- ½ cup (125 g) salt (kosher, rock salt, or regular table salt will do fine)
- 1 cup (250 ml) whipping cream or heavy (double) cream
- 2 tbsp white sugar
- Vanilla extract
- Sprinkles, gummies, cookie pieces, chocolate chips to sprinkle on top (optional)

Makes 2 servings

1 Half-fill the large re-sealable plastic bag with ice cubes, then add the salt.

2 In the smaller re-sealable plastic bag combine the cream, sugar, and a few drops of vanilla extract. Make sure you seal the smaller plastic bag really well.

The science

Adding salt to ice in an airtight container makes temperatures drop quickly. This makes the contents of the second container freeze faster. Ice cubes + salt = a freezing environment, which surrounds the bag of sugar and cream. Who knew making ice cream was so easy?!

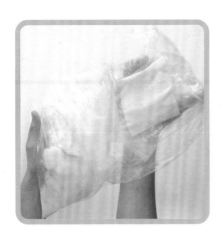

3 Put the smaller bag with the cream mixture inside the larger plastic bag. Now seal the large plastic bag.

4 Here's the fun part! For the next 5—8 minutes, constantly shake the bag. Shake! Shake! Shake! (You can also put the plastic bags in the freezer overnight should you be a lazy shaker!)

5 When the time is up (and the ice cream is the desired consistency—nice and creamy!) you are done. Eat and enjoy!

6 If you like, add sprinkles, gummies, cookie pieces, chocolate chips, or any other favorite ice cream toppings.

Guess What... ?
Ice

Ice is made when water is frozen. We use ice to cool drinks (ice cubes), to skate on (ice rink), and to make art (ice sculptures). Yearly, in Quebec, Canada, an ice hotel is built, made entirely from—you guessed it—ice! The famous ice hotel has an ice roof, ice walls, and ice floor along with ice furniture. Yes, you can even sleep overnight in an ice bed (cuddled up in a very warm sleeping bag, of course!).

English: ice
French: glace
Spanish: hielo

Chocolate Mug Cake

MAKE IT IN: **15 minutes**
BOREDOM BUSTER: **One time activity (but you can make it again and again)**
ACTIVITY LEVEL: ★ ★

This is the easiest chocolate cake you will ever make! The secret to this yummy recipe is the chocolate chips—don't forget to add them—and do use a BIG mug! This is a great recipe if you don't have the time or ingredients to make a big cake.

Things you need:

- A big coffee mug
- 4 tbsp all-purpose (plain) flour
- 4 tbsp white sugar
- 2 tbsp cocoa
- Spoon
- 1 egg
- 3 tbsp milk
- 3 tbsp cooking oil
- 3 tbsp chocolate chips
- Oven mitts

Makes 1 Mug Cake

Stop for safety!
Ask an adult to help you use the microwave.

1 In a large mug, measure and pour the dry ingredients—the flour, sugar, and cocoa—and mix them all together with a spoon.

2 Add the wet ingredients—the egg, milk, and oil—and mix well.

Serve this mug cake with a spoon for eating. The chocolate chips (you remembered to add them, right?!) will be soft and gooey inside the cake.

3 Now add the chocolate chips.

4 Put the mug in the microwave and heat, uncovered, for 2 minutes and 30 seconds on high. The cake will puff up in the microwave—but that's OK!

5 The cup and cake will be HOT, so put on oven mitts to take it out of the microwave. Let cool for 2 minutes. Enjoy!

Guess What...
Sugar

Sugar comes from the sugar cane plant. Sugar cane is generally grown in tropical (warm) climates like South and Central America, Australia, and the Caribbean. The sugar cane stalk can grow up to 19 feet (6 meters) high!

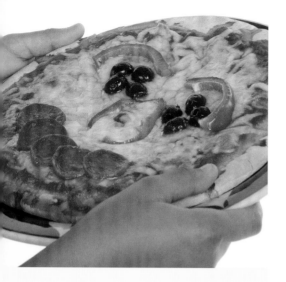

Pizza Face

All kids like pizza, right? OK—*most* kids like pizza. After-school snack, weeknight treat, or sleepover dinner, pizza can be a very kid-friendly food. In a few simple steps, you can take an ordinary pizza crust and turn it into a pizza face sure to entertain and appeal to the whole family.

MAKE IT IN: **25 minutes**
BOREDOM BUSTER: **One time activity (but you can make it again and again)**
ACTIVITY LEVEL: ★

1 Ask an adult to help you to turn the oven on to 350°F (180°C/Gas 4) to preheat.

Stop for safety!
Ask an adult to help you with the hot oven.

Things you need:

- 1 large ready-made pizza base or 4 individual ready-made pizza bases
- ½ cup (115 ml) tomato sauce (not ketchup!)
- 1 packet shredded mozzarella cheese
- Black olives
- Red bell pepper slices
- Pepperoni slices
- Cookie (baking) sheet
- Spoon

Serves 4

2 Put the pizza base on a cookie (baking) sheet. Using the back of a spoon, lightly spread tomato sauce all over the pizza base to cover it.

Guess What... Pizza

Pizza is one of Italy's most famous food creations. A pizza with crust, tomato sauce, and cheese is known as a "Margherita Pizza." It is said Margherita pizza was named in honor of Italy's Queen Margherita, in 1889, as it resembled the colors of the Italian flag—white cheese, red tomatoes, and topped with green basil.

3 Next, sprinkle a layer of shredded mozzarella cheese over the tomato sauce and put a few black olives in position to make the eyes of your pizza face.

4 Add slices of red bell pepper above the eyes as eyebrows, and in the center as a nose. Then put a few pepperoni slices in the shape of a smile.

5 Ask an adult to help you to put the cookie (baking) sheet in the oven and bake for 10 minutes, or as directed on the pizza base packet.

More pizza ideas:

For more flavors and faces, try using two tomato slices as eyes, a slice of mushroom for the nose, and a pepperoni slice for the mouth. Think about some other ingredients (which you may already have in your kitchen) that would taste great in this recipe—maybe some ham, sausage, onions, or spinach.

CHAPTER 5
Travel Activities

Wooden Spoon Puppets

Simple to make on-the-go, as well as easily packable, these Wooden Spoon Puppets are sure to bust the boredom of any trip. They are a great way to role-play a story, tell jokes, or even have Wooden Spoon Puppets sing-a-long with the car radio.

MAKE IT IN: 15 minutes
BOREDOM BUSTER: One time activity (but you can play with them over and over again)
ACTIVITY LEVEL: ★ ★

Things you need:

• A wooden spoon (available at discount stores)
• Felt-tipped pens or markers
• Pipe cleaners
• Googly eyes, yarn (for hair), glue, ribbon, or fabric scraps (optional)

1 Take a wooden spoon and draw a face (eyes, nose, mouth) on the inside.

2 On the back of the spoon, draw some hair.

Wooden Spoon Puppet story ideas:

• *Goldilocks and the Three Bears (one spoon Goldilocks, three spoons bears)*
• *Little Red Riding Hood (one spoon Little Red on front and Grandma on back and one spoon Wolf on front and Huntsman on back)*
• *Peter Pan and Captain Hook (one spoon Peter, one spoon Hook)*

3 Next, position a piece of pipe cleaner centered beneath the spoon handle and then wrap it around the handle twice to make puppet arms.

4 It's that easy! You can decorate your puppet further with googly eyes, glue on pieces of yarn for hair (you can make braids), and even make a scarf from ribbon or fabric strips.

Guess What...
Pipe Cleaners

Pipe cleaners are lengths of wire covered with bristles. Originally, pipe cleaners were used specifically to clean pipes (hence the name!). They can still be used to clean or unplug tight places. Pipe cleaners are a very popular craft supply because of their flexibility.

T-shirt Travel Pillow

A travel pillow is handy to have while you are traveling, giving you a comfy place to lay your head when you need a snooze. Simple and easy, this travel pillow can go anywhere with you—a sleepover, car trip, vacation, or even just to use at home! This activity is really easy and you don't even need to sew!

Turn an old T-shirt into something comfy!

MAKE IT IN: **45 minutes**
BOREDOM BUSTER: **One time activity (but you can use it forever)**
ACTIVITY LEVEL: ★ ★

Things you need:

- A clean T-shirt (one that you have grown out of is ideal)
- Ruler
- Chalk (any color)
- Scissors: fabric scissors work best
- Pillow stuffing: you could use cotton balls, cotton stuffing, mismatched old socks, or clean rags

1 Put your T-shirt on a flat surface. Using your ruler, measure a rectangle from just below the neck to just above the bottom hem. (If there is a picture or wording on your T-shirt, be sure to measure around it). Using chalk, mark the straight lines of this rectangle—it will wipe or brush off when you are done.

2 Holding the top and bottom layers of the T-shirt together, use your scissors to cut out the rectangle.

3 Next, measure another rectangle about 1½–2in (4–5cm) inside the first rectangle and, using chalk, mark it on the fabric.

4 Next, holding the top and bottom layers of the T-shirt together, snip along the edge of the T-shirt to just beyond the marked line, making cuts about 1in (2.5cm) apart, creating strips. Do this to all four sides of the T-shirt.

5 Starting at one corner, take a top layer strip and double knot it to the matching bottom layer strip. Double knot three sides of the T-shirt Travel Pillow.

6 Finally, put stuffing into the open end of the travel pillow, then double knot the fourth side to close it when the pillow is soft and comfy. Brush off the chalk marks and you're done!

Guess What...
Pillows

In 1922, the tomb of King Tutankhamun, a boy king of Egypt who ruled more than three thousand years ago, was discovered. He is often referred to as "King Tut." Discovered in his tomb were hundreds of objects fit for a king. One of these was a headrest carved out of elephant ivory. King Tut would use it to rest his head upon instead of using a pillow.

T-shirt Infinity Scarf

The air-conditioning in airplanes, trains, and cars can be chilly, making for an uncomfortable journey. Cuddle up in this easy, no-sew activity! This T-shirt Infinity Scarf packs very compactly so you can throw it in your activity bag or tie it on your backpack with ease.

Reinvent your outgrown clothes as cool accessories.

MAKE IT IN: **5 minutes**
BOREDOM BUSTER: **One time activity (but you can wear it forever)**
ACTIVITY LEVEL: ★

Things you need:

- A clean, old T-shirt
- Scissors: fabric scissors work best

You can make several, different colored, T-shirt Infinity Scarves and layer them for a sleek and stylish look.

1 Lay your T-shirt out on a flat surface. Cut off the bottom hem from the front and back—use the stitching on the hem as a guide but don't worry too much about cutting a straight line because the cotton fabric from the T-shirt will roll a bit at the cut edges to hide any jagged cuts. Put the hem aside (you don't need it for this activity).

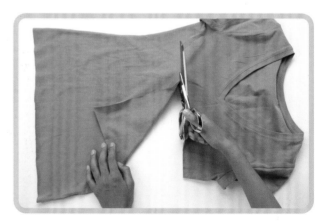

2 From the bottom of your T-shirt, measure three-quarters of the way up—you don't need a tape measure to do this, you can estimate or just cut across under the arms. Cut through both layers (the top and bottom) at the three-quarter mark. (If there is a graphic on the T-shirt, cut under it.)

3 Put aside the top portion of the T-shirt, including the arm and neck portions. See step 6 for tips on other things to make with these.

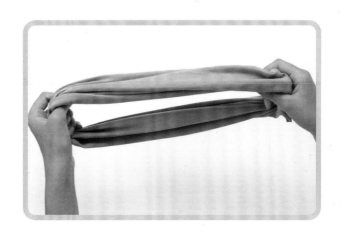

4 The main part of T-shirt material will be one long band of fabric—this is the T-shirt Infinity Scarf! Using your hands, stretch the fabric. Gently pull and lightly tug until it is as long as you would like for a scarf.

5 Loop the T-shirt Infinity Scarf around your neck—make a double loop if it's long enough. Done!

Guess What...
Infinity

Infinity means something that is endless. When something does not have a starting point or an ending point—like a circle—it goes on for infinity.

6 You can use the leftover bits of T-shirt fabric from the arms to make an infinity necklace. Cut across the arms to make small circles. Thread them together by looping one through the other and fasten by tying the last two together.

Travel Journal

Writing is a great way of recording traveling adventures and experiences. A Travel Journal only takes minutes to make, using materials you already have in your house or classroom! Use a map for the cover and draw your route on it. Alternatively, make it with a plain cover, then decorate it with mementos, such as photos, tickets, and postcards.

MAKE IT IN: **15 minutes**
BOREDOM BUSTER: **One time activity (but you can write in it again and again)**
ACTIVITY LEVEL: ★★

Things you need:

- 5 sheets of standard size paper
- 1 piece of standard size card (if you don't have card stock cut a piece of cereal box cardboard to a standard size instead)
- Map (use an old map or print one from the computer)
- Pencil
- Scissors
- Glue
- Hole punch
- String, yarn, or ribbon

1 Stack the five sheets of paper together and fold them in half, top to bottom. Press your finger along the fold to make a crease in the paper. It already looks like a book!

2 Put a piece of card on your map and draw around the edge with a pencil. Then cut out the marked section of the map with scissors.

Guess What... Map of the World

Look at a map of the world and you will see the continents. A "continent" is a very large land mass on planet Earth. The five continents, where people live, are Africa, Eurasia (which includes Europe and Asia together), America (which includes North America and South America together), Antarctica, and Australia.

The five rings of the modern Olympic Games represent the five continents. The rings are interlaced to show the athletes coming together to compete in the games.

3 Now glue the map onto the card or cereal cardboard. When the glue is dry, fold the map from top to bottom to match the inside pages and press your finger along the card fold to make a crease.

4 Open the five sheets of paper so they lie flat. Using the hole punch, punch a hole at the top and a hole at the bottom in the crease of the paper, about 1in (2.5cm) in from the edge.

5 Now open out the card and place the sheets of paper on top, on the inside, and line them up so the paper is straight. Using your pencil, mark where the holes are through the pages.

6 Take the paper pages away, line up the hole punch on the pencil marks, and punch two holes, in the top and bottom of the card.

7 Cut a length of string about 24in (60cm) long and thread it through each of the holes. Tie a bow or knot with the string on the outside of the Travel Journal. Done!

Felt Story Board

Give a new purpose to an old cereal box.

MAKE IT IN: **15 minutes**
BOREDOM BUSTER: **One time activity (but you can use it again and again)**
ACTIVITY LEVEL: ★ ★

Things you need:

- Cardboard rectangle (re-use an old cereal box or the spare piece from the **Cereal Box Travel Desk** on page 126)
- Scissors
- Sheets of felt in 2 or more colors
- Marker pen
- White PVA glue
- Round objects, like a tape roll, for outlining round shapes
- Ruler for outlining square, triangle, and rectangle shapes

This activity was invented when going through the odds and ends left in our art area. Some felt, some leftover cardboard, and some glue provided all the inspiration needed to create a Felt Story Board. This is great when traveling, as felt sticks to felt (meaning the pieces will stay in place!). All you need is your imagination!

1 Using scissors, cut out a cardboard rectangle. You can make it any size: try drawing around a piece of standard paper, or cutting out the side of a cereal box.

2 Take a piece of felt and cut it to the size of the cardboard rectangle. Put the cardboard on top of the felt and draw around it, then cut out the felt.

3 Apply some glue to the felt and stick it to the blank (inside) side of the cardboard.

4 Using a tape roll as your guide, draw circles on the second color of felt—draw around the outside and inside of the roll to get different sizes, or use other round objects, like buttons or a plastic cup or lid, to draw around.

5 Using a ruler as your guide, mark squares, triangles, and rectangles on another piece of felt.

Put the Felt Story Board inside your Cereal Box Travel Desk (see page 126) for easy storage on car trips.

(see page 126)

Guess What...
Felt

Felt is a fabric often made from wool, recycled plastic fibers (some felts are made from recycled plastic bottles!), and man-made materials. Felts can come in a rainbow of vivid colors. Felt is a popular craft supply but it is also used for many other things: clothing, computer sleeves, baby shoes, hats, bags, and ornaments.

6 Cut out all the felt shapes and arrange them on your board in different patterns. It's that easy!

Cryptograms

Cryptograms are a type of puzzle solved by cracking a code. The secret is to replace alphabet letters with numbers or shapes. You can make a cryptogram and use it for secret codes for notes between friends or travel companions, or just to keep your ideas, adventures, and personal stuff hush-hush! This is a fantastic, quiet activity that works your brain.

MAKE IT IN: **5 minutes**
BOREDOM BUSTER: **You can play this over and over again**
ACTIVITY LEVEL: ★

Things you need:

• Cryptogram code
• Paper or notebook
• Pencil

1 Write out your cryptogram code on a sheet of paper or in your notebook. Start with the alphabet from A to Z: under each letter write a number from 1 to 26, in any order.

2 Then, on another sheet of paper or page, write out a coded message. Show the code only to people with whom you want to share secret messages!

3 Done! Who will crack your code?!

Create secret messages using your code:

I	S	E	E	Y	O	U!
18	8	22	22	2	12	6!

Fortune Teller

This paper game is fun to play on your own or with friends and classmates. This is a paper folding activity, and is sometimes called a Cootie Catcher (you can use it as a pincer to capture cooties!). Personalize the decorations and fortunes as you like—you can even use them as birthday party invitations!

MAKE IT IN: **15 minutes**
BOREDOM BUSTER: **One time activity (but you can play with it again and again)**
ACTIVITY LEVEL: ★ ★ ★

Things you need:

- One standard size piece of paper in any color
- Scissors: see the box below if you don't have scissors

1 Place your sheet of paper on a flat surface. Fold the paper into a triangle by taking one corner and folding it diagonally across the paper, lining it up with the straight line on the outer edge.

2 Cut off the remaining rectangle at the top (you can re-use it as a bookmark).

No scissors? No problem! Fold your paper really well. Then, use your fingernail to press a crease into the paper. Next, take something straight—a ruler or a book—and put it on one side of the crease. Now gently rip the paper along the edge with your fingers.

3 Now you have a triangle. Run your finger along the fold to make a crease, then open out the triangle (you now have a square).

Decorating ideas:

Colors on the outside:
Red, Blue, Yellow, Red

Numbers on the inside:
1 through 8

8 Fortunes on the flipside:

- *I don't think*
- *Maybe tomorrow*
- *Ask again later*
- *Yes*
- *I think so*
- *No way*
- *Absolutely*
- *Not today*

4 Fold your paper in the opposite direction so that you make a triangle going the other way. Make a crease and open out the paper. Now you will have two creases in your paper (which cross at exactly the center point).

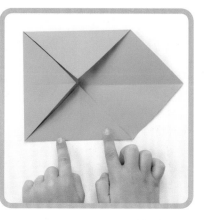

5 With your paper as a square, take one corner and fold it into the center so that the corner point meets the center point. Repeat with the other three corners.

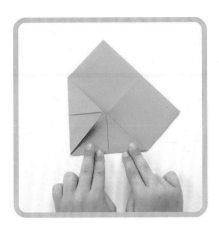

6 Flip your paper over. Repeat step 5, folding each corner into the center of the square. You will end up with many triangles within the square.

7 Fold the paper in half. Put your fingers in the bottom of the triangles and push up gently. The Fortune Teller folding is done.

8 Lift up the flaps of the Fortune Teller and decorate inside them!

How to play:

- Ask the fortune teller a question. "Will I meet someone famous?"
- Choose a color and spell it out: R-E-D.
- Choose a number: open and close the Fortune Teller the number of times you chose: ONE-TWO-THREE-FOUR.
- Choose another number and flip the Fortune Teller over to reveal the answer to the question you asked: "Not today!"

Cereal Box Travel Desk

This Cereal Box Travel Desk is two activities in one. Make the travel desk ahead of your trip (activity #1) and then use it on your voyage (activity #2). The cereal box lays flat on your lap, making it an easy and inexpensive travel desk. It's great to keep your cars, snacks, toys, games, or crayons from falling under your feet while you are on a road trip.

Old cereal boxes can make great desks to play with on long journeys.

MAKE IT IN: 45 minutes
BOREDOM BUSTER: One time activity (but you can use it again and again)
ACTIVITY LEVEL: ★ ★ ★

Things you need:

- A large, family-sized cereal box
- Scissors
- Ruler
- Marker pens
- Duct tape (optional)

1 Put the cereal box on your work surface. Using one blade of the scissors, carefully score the outside top rectangle of the cereal box (score means to mark a line along the cardboard using your scissors, but not to cut all the way through).

2 Carefully push the scissors through the scored line and cut along the lines, removing the outside top rectangle of the cereal box.

Guess What... Cardboard

Cardboard is made of heavy-duty paper. Cardboard can be used for business cards, cereal boxes, postcards, playing cards, TV boxes, and more! You can even buy furniture made out of cardboard (it's an eco-friendly building supply!).

English: cardboard box
French: boîte en carton
Spanish : caja de cartón

3 Use the scissors carefully to neaten the edges of the Cereal Box Travel Desk. Set aside the cut-away cardboard rectangle in your art area (you can re-use it to make the Felt Story Board activity on page 120).

4 Using a ruler and marker pens, draw on the inside of the travel desk—see the box below for ideas on what to draw. If you like, using scissors, cut pieces of duct tape to cover the bottom and sides of your Cereal Box Travel Desk to cover up the cereal pictures.

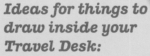

Stop for safety!
Ask an adult to help with cutting.

Ideas for things to draw inside your Travel Desk:

- *Road lines or train tracks*
- *A house with rooms*
- *A city with buildings, parks, and roads*
- *A school with classrooms and desks*
- *A map to track your travels*
- *Leave it blank and use it as a work surface for coloring*

Index